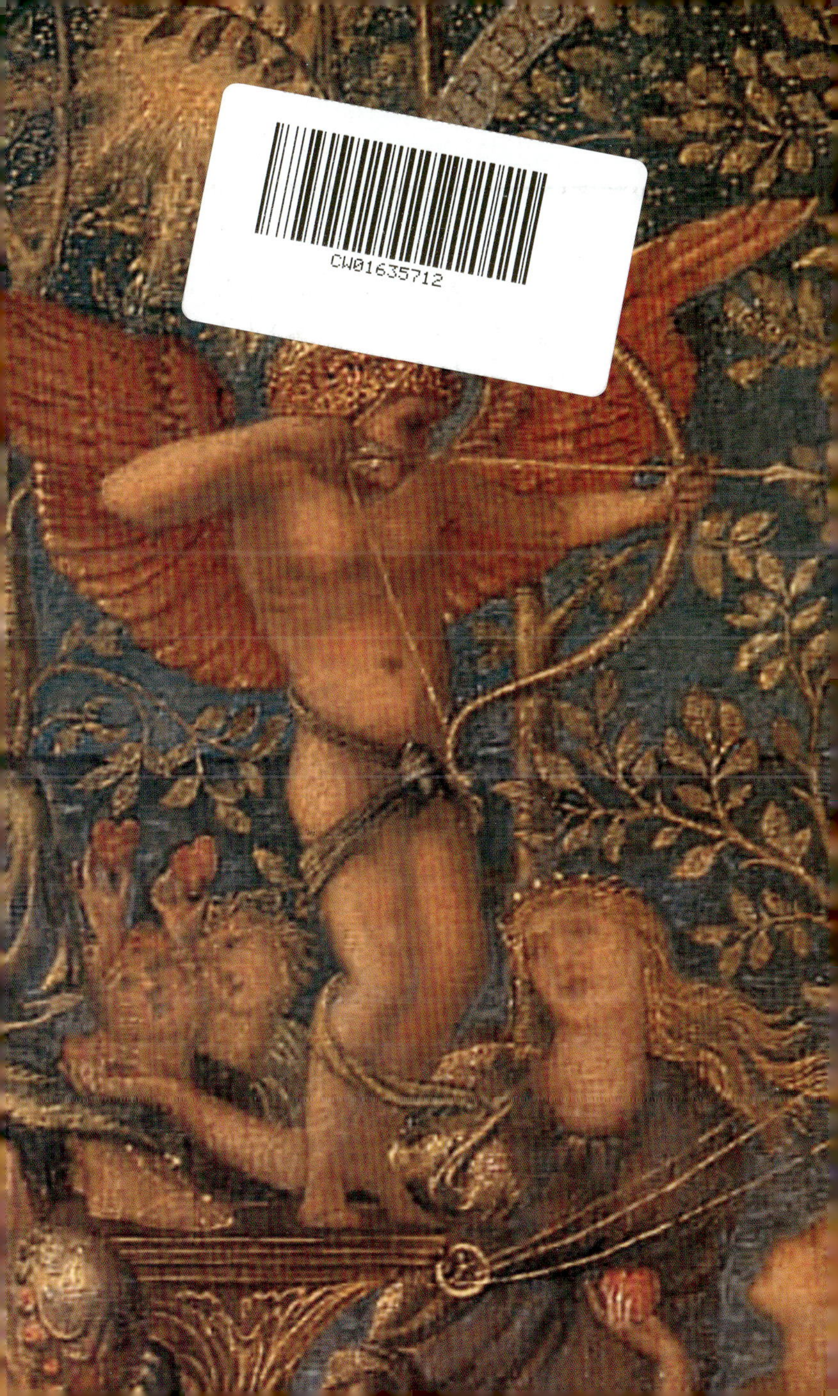

Love is Enough: Pre-Raphaelite Paintings and Poems

Special Edition for PAST TIMES ®, Oxford, England
First published in Great Britain in 1998 by
Frances Lincoln Limited, 4 Torriano Mews
Torriano Avenue, London NW5 2RZ

For photographic acknowledgements and copyright details,
see pages 86-91 and page 93

British Library Cataloguing in Publication Data
available on request.

ISBN 0-7112-1369-0

Set by MATS, Southend-on-Sea, Essex
Designed by David Fordham

Printed in Hong Kong

1 3 5 7 9 8 6 4 2

Love is Enough

~ Pre-Raphaelite Paintings and Poems ~

With an introduction by Clive Wilmer

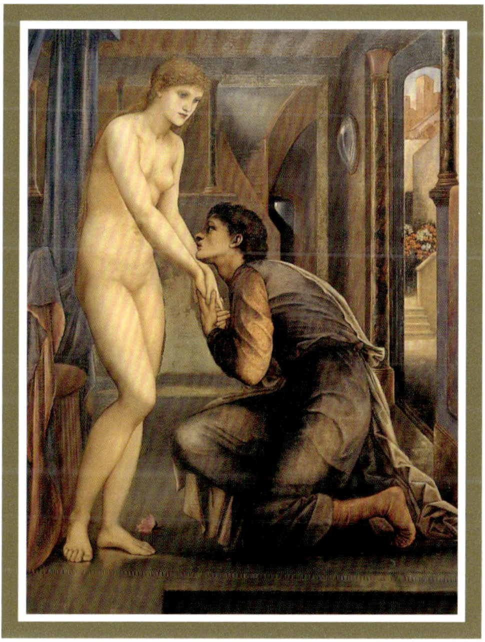

PAST TIMES®

Introduction

For the artists and writers who formed the Pre-Raphaelite Brotherhood, all the arts were one: their inspiration as artists was often literary and they sometimes wrote new poems to go with their paintings. This book records several of these connections, as well as inventing new ones.

The theme of the book is love. In its own day, Pre-Raphaelite love poetry was accused of 'fleshliness'. Today the more likely charge is idealisation, but neither judgement quite meets the case. Love is nothing if not physical, but it is also something more. What most preoccupied these poets and painters was love as dream, obsession, longing, even nightmare.

The Brotherhood was founded in 1848. A secret society of youthful painters, rebels against a stuffy art establishment, they valued the freshness of pre-Renaissance painting. The key figures were William Holman Hunt, John Everett Millais and Dante Gabriel Rossetti. They admired all things medieval. Rossetti, in particular, championed the work of Dante Alighieri, especially his love poems, which he translated and illustrated. They also had modern enthusiasms: Romantic poets such as Keats, Shelley and Byron, all recently dead, provided them with subjects for their paintings, as did more recent poets like Alfred Tennyson.

Hunt, Millais and Rossetti soon went their separate ways but before long, a second phase of the movement was underway with Rossetti at its centre. The new brothers, who began as Rossetti's disciples, were Edward Burne-Jones, eventually to surpass him as a painter, and William Morris, soon to be famous as poet, designer, businessman and political activist.

At this stage, Morris was struggling to be a painter. When he met his future wife, the exotically beautiful Jane Burden, he painted her as Sir Tristram's love, Iseult. Tongue-tied in the presence of beauty and frustrated by his tussle with paint and canvas, he scrawled a note on the back of his half-finished picture: "I cannot paint you," it said, "but I love you." At the same time, with more confidence, he wrote Jane the poem *Praise of my Lady*.

Unfortunately Rossetti too loved Jane, and he not only could paint her but did so obsessively. His picture of her as *Proserpine*, goddess of spring, reveals her as a woman doomed to spend half the year in darkness – that is, with a husband she could not love. The poem *Proserpine* points cryptically to the picture's significance.

Jane was not the only woman in Rossetti's life. He painted Elizabeth Siddal just as obsessively and married her after a ten-year engagement. Her death from an overdose of laudanum oppressed Rossetti with guilt for the rest of his life; it inspired the painting *Beata Beatrix*, which equates her with Dante's dead love, Beatrice. Rossetti also enjoyed coarser women. His 'housekeeper' Fanny Cornforth, a former prostitute, was the model for *Lady Lilith* and several other paintings.

Problems of the heart were endemic to the Pre-Raphaelite circle. Georgiana Burne-Jones provided the lonely Morris with consolation, only to find herself in need of it when her husband fell in love with Maria Zambaco, a Greek beauty who modelled for some of his paintings. The pain and guilt of such situations is at the root of Pre-Raphaelite melancholy.

Much Pre-Raphaelite work is ethereally beautiful in ways the modern world finds difficult, although much of it is also sensual. Dream-like as it is, it grew out of real circumstances, and dreams are always real to those who dream them. Christina Rossetti saw this with an objectivity denied to her brother. In her sonnet *In An Artist's Studio*, she says of his images of Elizabeth Siddal,

> *"Not as she is, but was when hope shone bright:*
> *Not as she is, but as she fills his dream."*

There is a touch of acerbity in these lines, but it is more at the expense of morbid obsession than anything one could call idealisation.

Indeed, Elizabeth Siddal and Jane Morris would not have been much admired in the 1850s. Tall, pale, melancholy women in awkward, inelegant poses were very far from Victorian standards of beauty. What is more, like most Pre-Raphaelite models, they came from poor and deprived backgrounds and so were unfamiliar with orthodox fashion – a fact alluded to by Burne-Jones, perhaps, in his *King Cophetua and the Beggar Maid*. If such pictures and the poems that go with them strike us today as idealised, this is largely because they have helped to create our own idea of the beautiful.

Love-Lily

Dante Gabriel Rossetti

Between the hands, between the brows,
  Between the lips of Love-Lily,
A spirit is born whose birth endows
  My blood with fire to burn through me;
Who breathes upon my gazing eyes,
  Who laughs and murmurs in mine ear,
At whose least touch my colour flies,
  And whom my life grows faint to hear.

Within the voice, within the heart,
  Within the mind of Love-Lily,
A spirit is born who lifts apart
  His tremulous wings and looks at me;
Who on my mouth his finger lays,
  And shows, while whispering lutes confer,
That Eden of Love's watered ways
  Whose winds and spirits worship her.

Brows, hands, and lips, heart, mind, and voice,
  Kisses and words of Love-Lily,—
Oh! bid me with your joy rejoice
  Till riotous longing rest in me!
Ah! let not hope be still distraught,
  But find in her its gracious goal,
Whose speech Truth knows not from her thought
  Nor Love her body from her soul.

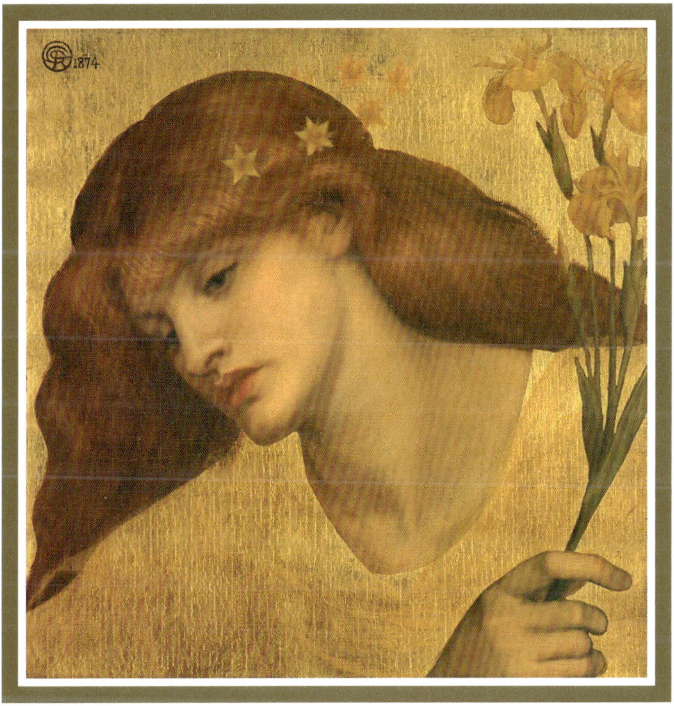
1874

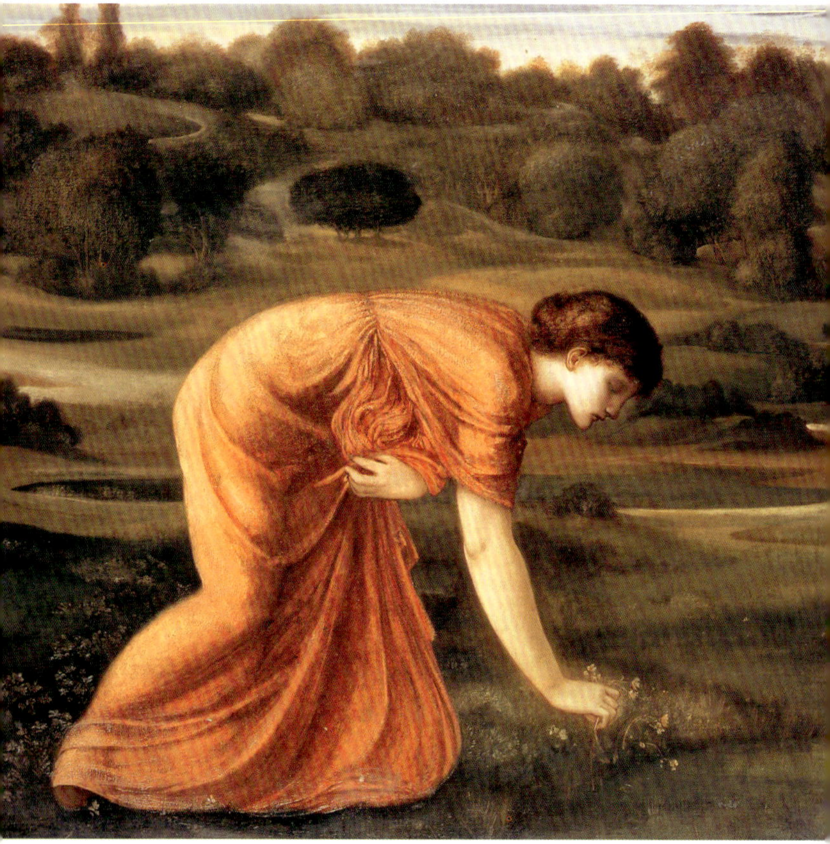

The Lost Love

William Wordsworth

She dwelt among the untrodden ways
Beside the springs of Dove;
A maid whom there were none to praise,
And very few to love.

A violet by a mossy stone
Half-hidden from the eye!
—Fair as a star, when only one
Is shining in the sky.

She lived unknown, and few could know
When Lucy ceased to be;
But she is in her grave, and O!
The difference to me!

~ Music, ~
When Soft Voices Die

Percy Bysshe Shelley

Music, when soft voices die,
Vibrates in the memory;
Odours, when sweet violets sicken,
Live within the sense they quicken.

Rose leaves, when the rose is dead,
Are heaped for the belovèd's bed;
And so thy thoughts, when thou art gone,
Love itself shall slumber on.

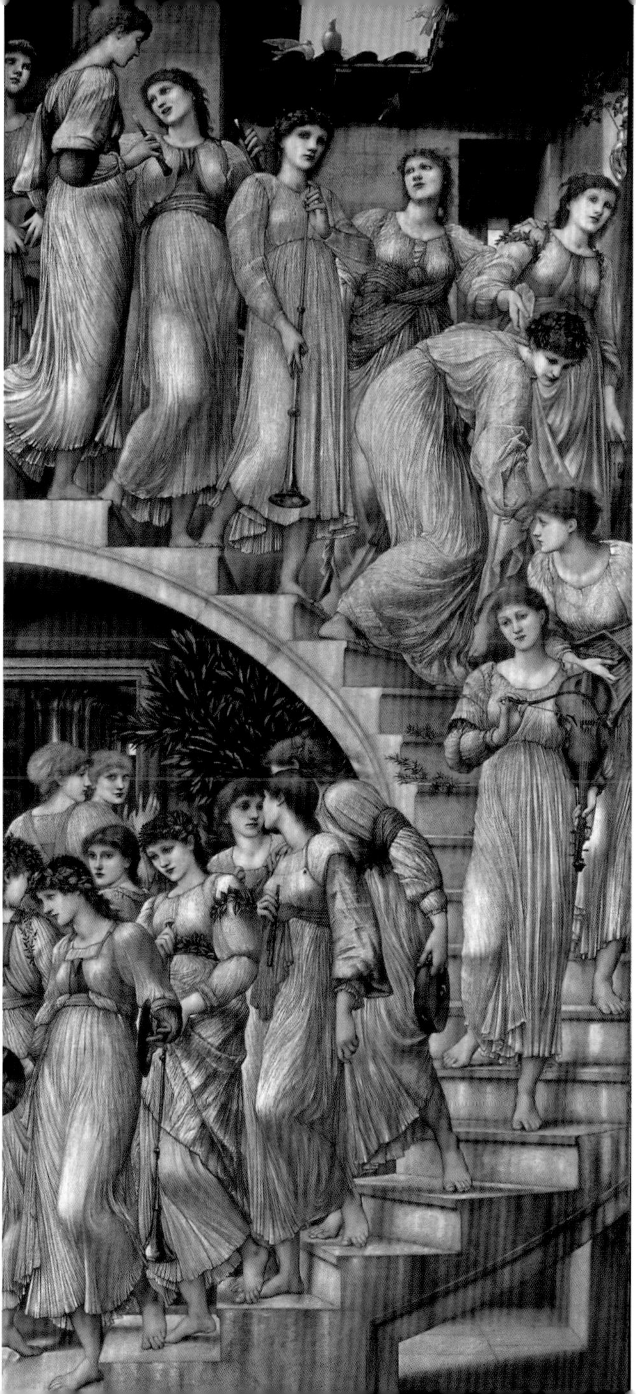

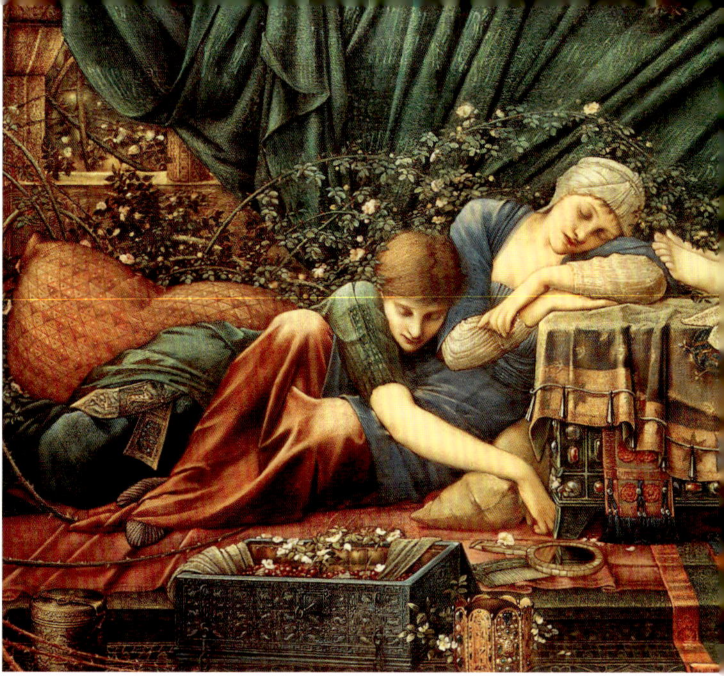

~For the Briar Rose~

William Morris

THE BRIARWOOD

The fateful slumber floats and flows
About the tangle of the rose;
But lo! the fated hand and heart
To rend the slumbrous curse apart!

THE COUNCIL ROOM

The threat of war, the hope of peace,
The Kingdom's peril and increase
Sleep on and bide the latter day,
When fate shall take her chain away.

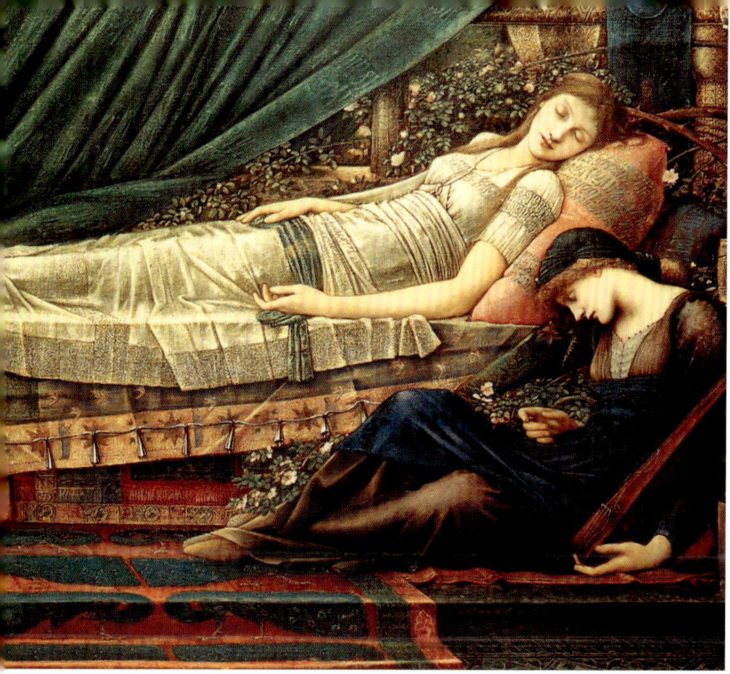

THE GARDEN COURT

The maiden pleasance of the land
Knoweth no stir of voice or hand,
No cup the sleeping waters fill,
The restless shuttle lieth still.

THE ROSEBOWER

Here lies the hoarded love, the key
To all the treasure that shall be;
Come fated hand the gift to take,
And smite this sleeping world awake.

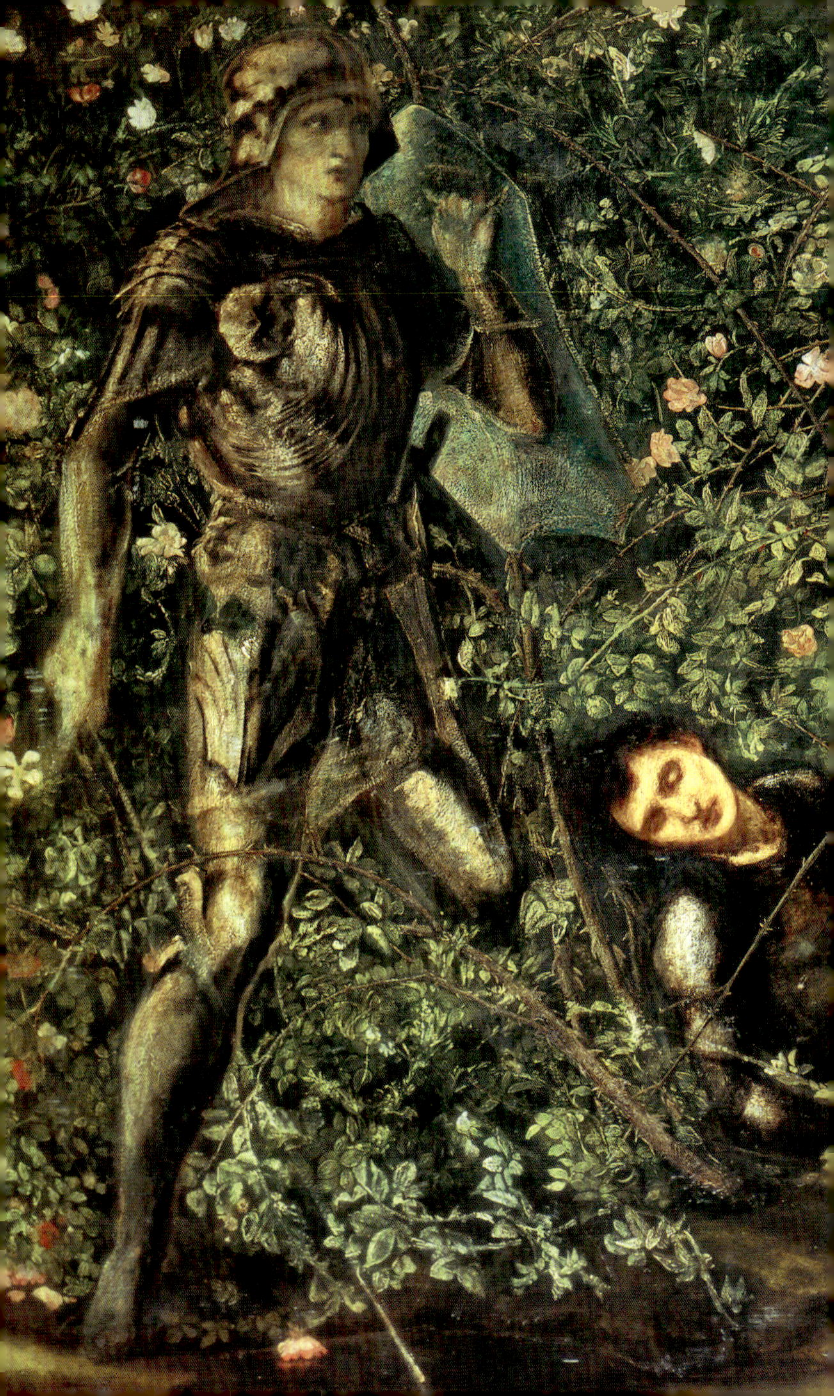

Another for the Briar Rose

William Morris

O treacherous scent, O thorny sight,
O tangle of world's wrong and right,
What art thou 'gainst my armour's gleam
But dusky cobwebs of a dream?

Beat down, deep sunk from every gleam
Of hope, they lie and dully dream;
Men once, but men no more, that Love
Their waste defeated hearts should move.

Here sleeps the world that would not love!
Let it sleep on, but if He move
Their hearts in humble wise to wait
On his new-wakened fair estate.

O won at last is never late!
Thy silence was the voice of fate;
Thy still hands conquered in the strife;
Thine eyes were light; thy lips were life.

from

THE PRINCESS

ALFRED TENNYSON

Now sleeps the crimson petal, now the white;
Nor waves the cypress in the palace walk;
Nor winks the gold fin in the porphyry font:
The fire-fly wakens: waken thou with me.

Now droops the milkwhite peacock like a ghost,
And like a ghost she glimmers on to me.

Now lies the Earth all Danaë to the stars,
And all thy heart lies open unto me.

Now slides the silent meteor on, and leaves
A shining furrow, as thy thoughts in me.

Now folds the lily all her sweetness up,
And slips into the bosom of the lake:
So fold thyself, my dearest, thou, and slip
Into my bosom and be lost in me.

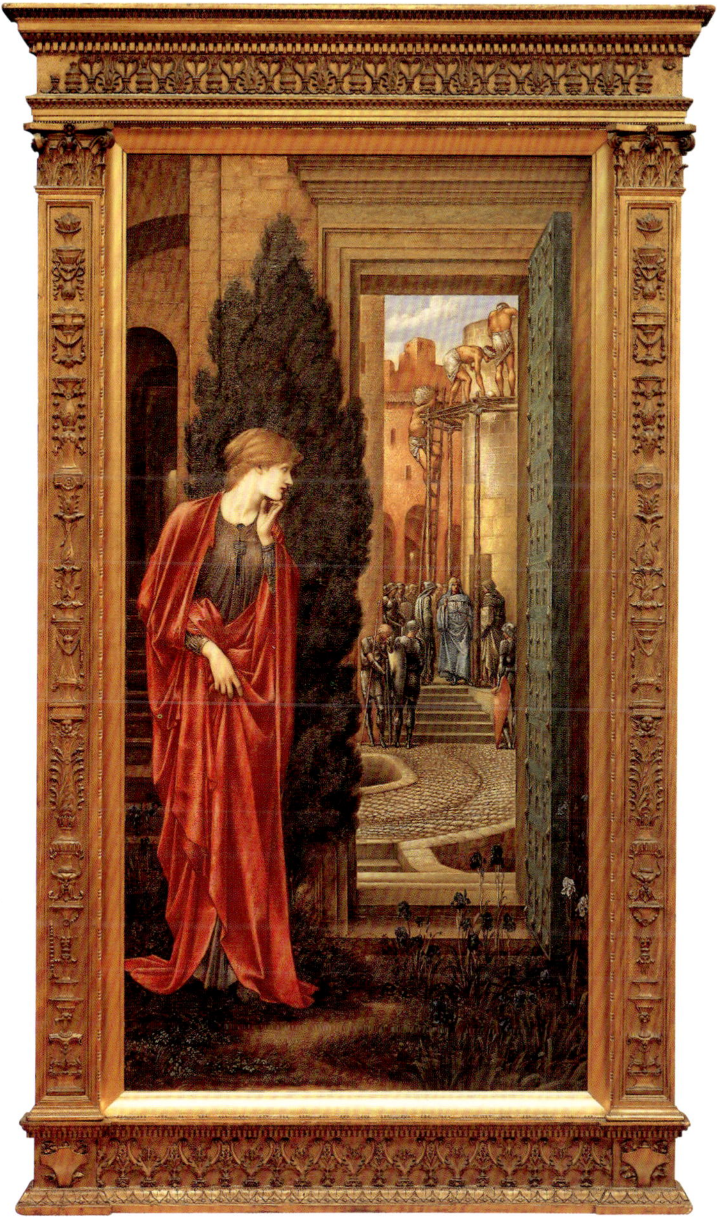

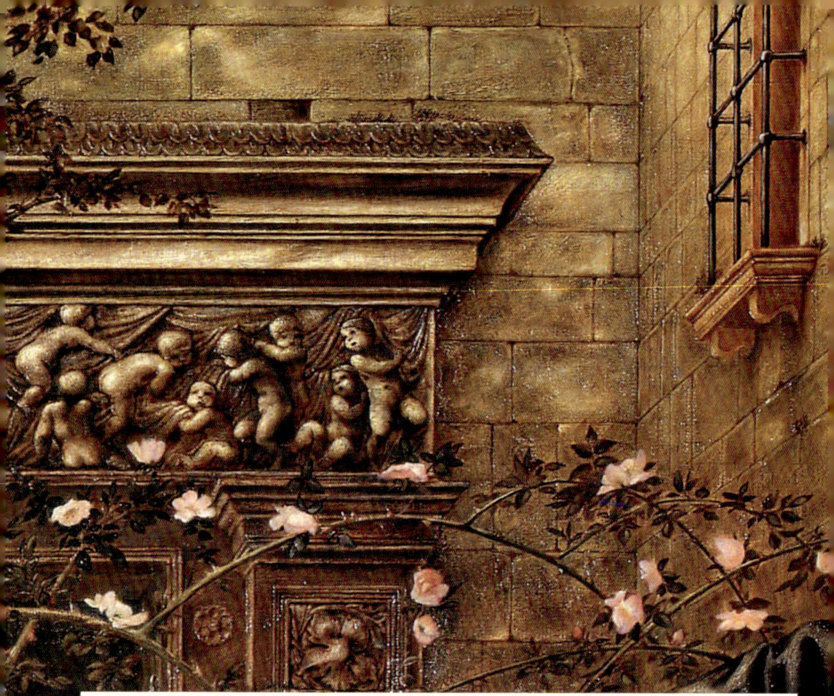

~ Love is Enough ~

William Morris

Love is enough: though the World be a-waning,
And the woods have no voice but the voice of complaining,
Though the sky be too dark for dim eyes to discover
The gold-cups and daisies fair blooming thereunder,
Though the hills be held shadows, and the sea a dark wonder
And this day draw a veil over all deeds passed over,
Yet their hands shall not tremble, their feet shall not falter;
The void shall not weary, the fear shall not alter
These lips and these eyes of the loved and the lover.

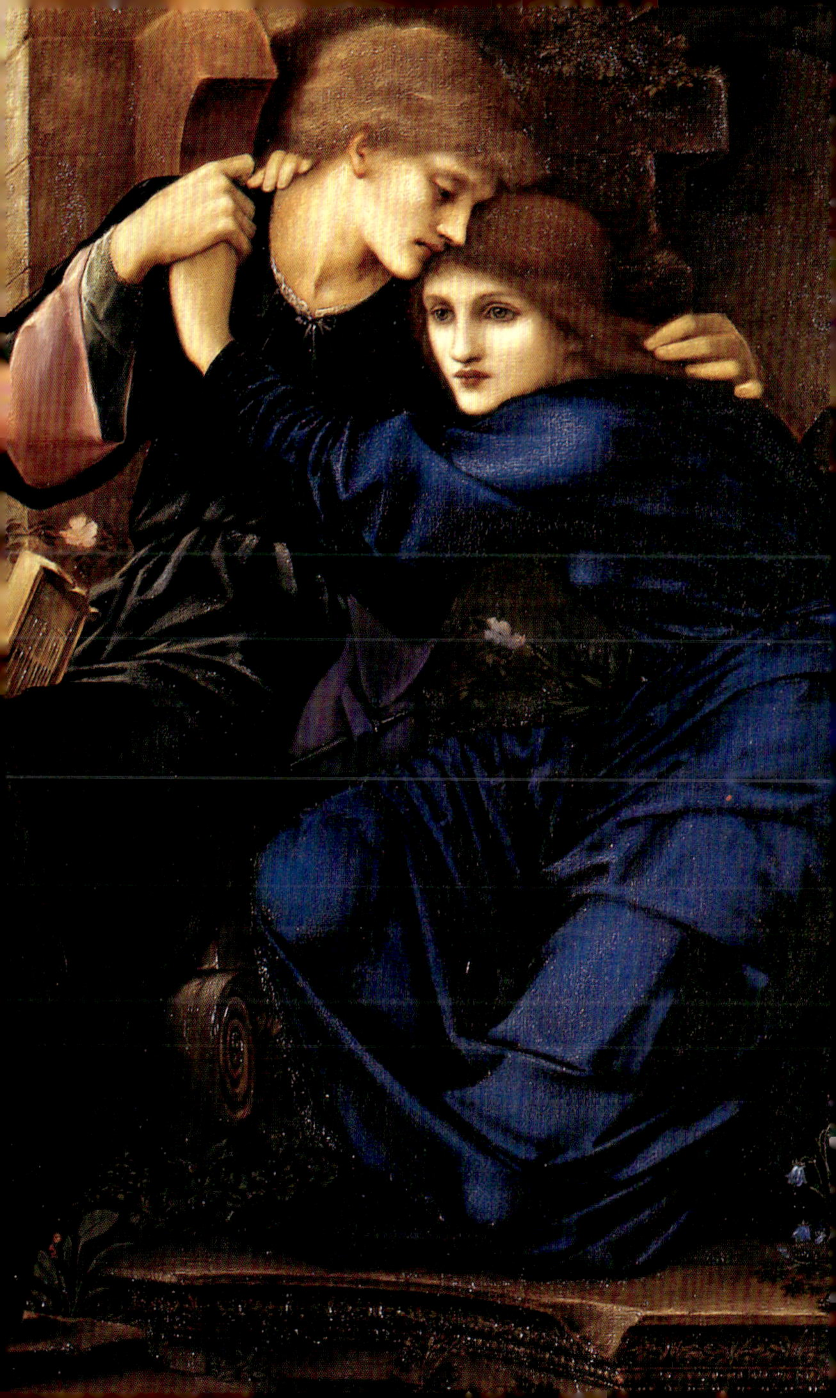

~ Body's Beauty ~

Dante Gabriel Rossetti

Of Adam's first wife, Lilith, it is told
  (The witch he loved before the gift of Eve)
  That, ere the snake's, her sweet tongue could deceive,
And her enchanted hair was the first gold.
And still she sits, young while the earth is old,
  And, subtly of herself contemplative,
  Draws men to watch the bright web she can weave,
Till heart and body and life are in its hold.

The rose and poppy are her flowers; for where
  Is he not found, O Lilith, whom shed scent
And soft-shed kisses and soft sleep shall snare?
  Lo! As that youth's eyes burned at thine, so went
  Thy spell through him, and left his straight neck bent
And round his heart one strangling golden hair.

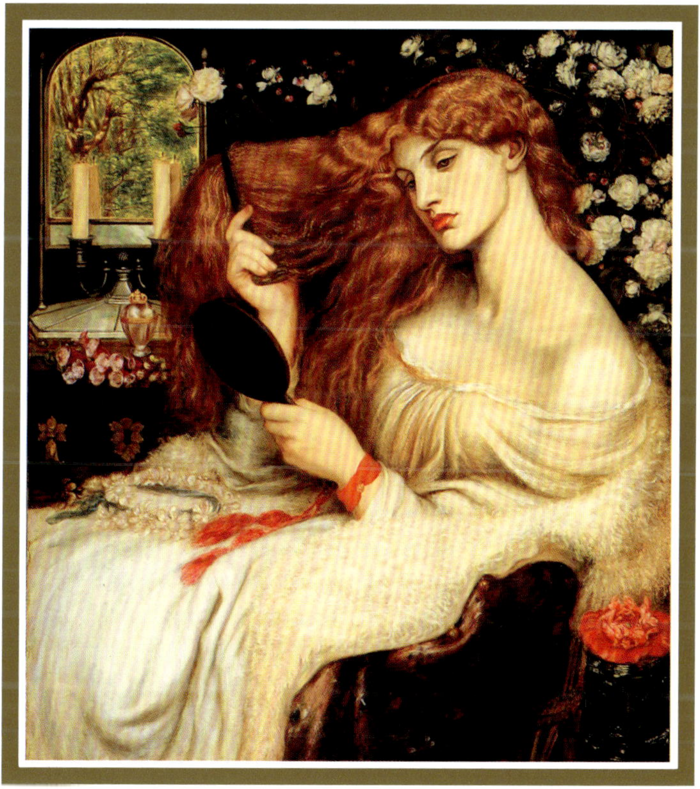

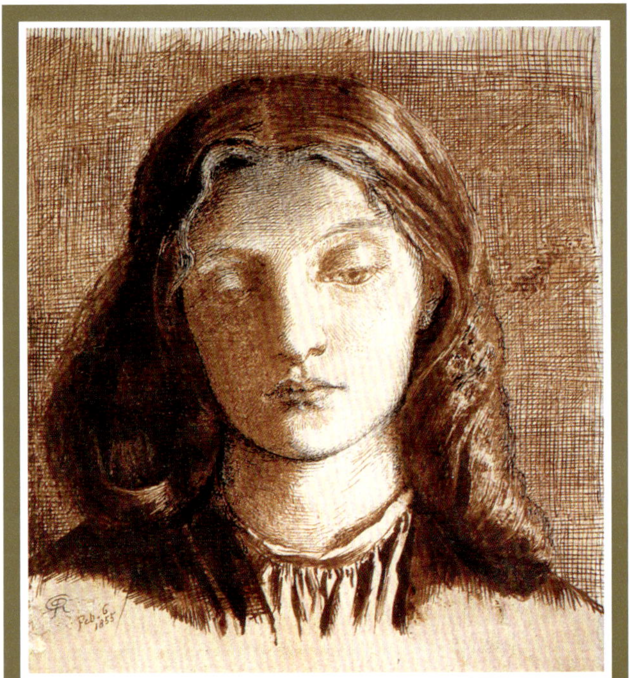
Feb. 6 1855

In an Artist's Studio

Christina Rossetti

One face looks out from all his canvases,
   One selfsame figure sits or walks or leans:
   We found her hidden just behind those screens,
That mirror gave back all her loveliness.
A queen in opal or in ruby dress,
   A nameless girl in freshest summer-greens,
   A saint, an angel—every canvas means
The same one meaning, neither more nor less.
He feeds upon her face by day and night,
   And she with true kind eyes looks back on him,
Fair as the moon and joyful as the light:
   Not wan with waiting, not with sorrow dim;
Not as she is, but was when hope shone bright;
   Not as she is, but as she fills his dream.

from

~ IDYLLS OF THE KING ~

ALFRED TENNYSON

In Love, if Love be Love, if Love be ours,
Faith and unfaith can ne'er be equal powers:
Unfaith in aught is want of faith in all.

It is the little rift within the lute,
That by and by will make the music mute,
And ever widening slowly silence all.

The little rift within the lover's lute
Or little pitted speck in garnered fruit,
That rotting inward slowly moulders all.

It is not worth the keeping: let it go:
But shall it? answer, darling, answer, no.
And trust me not at all or all in all.

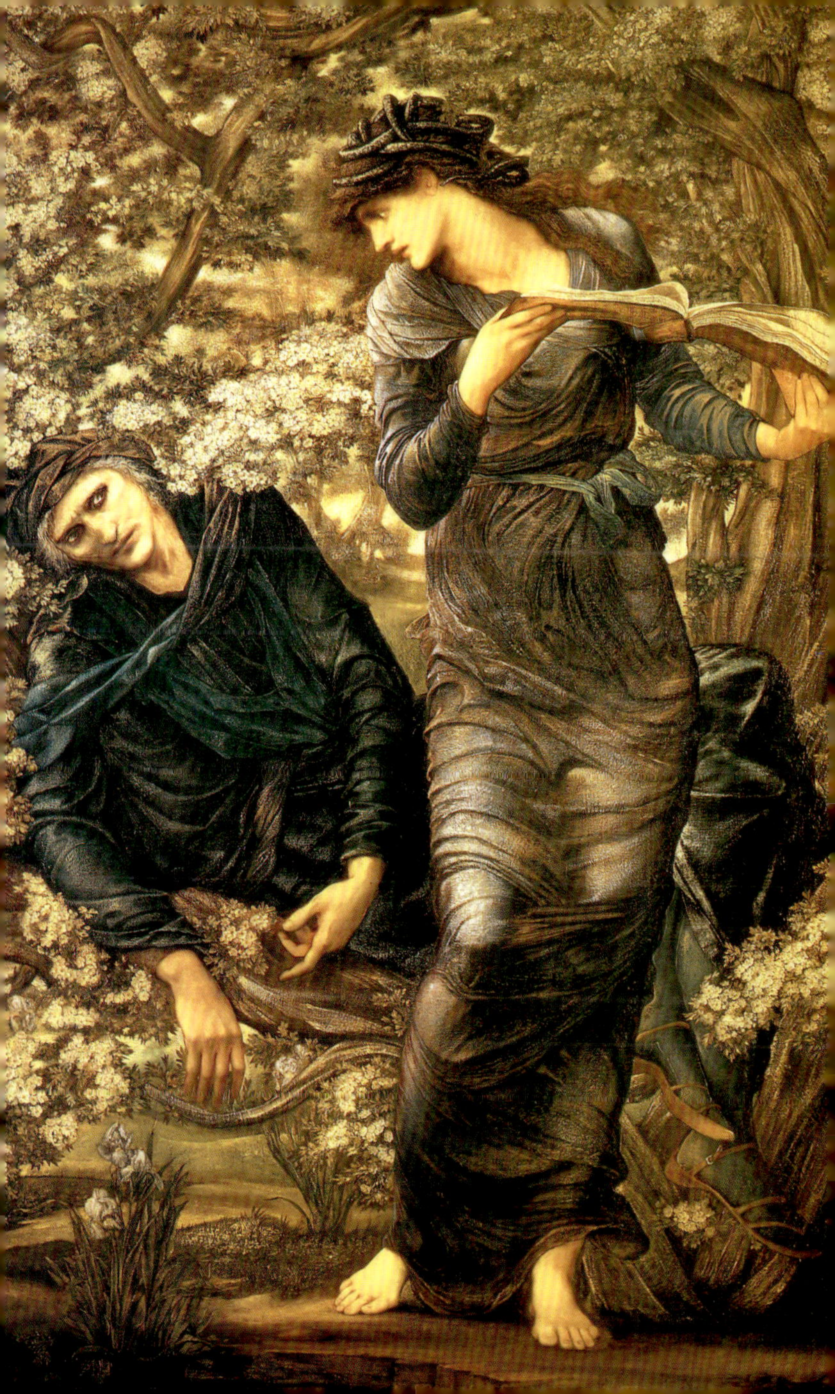

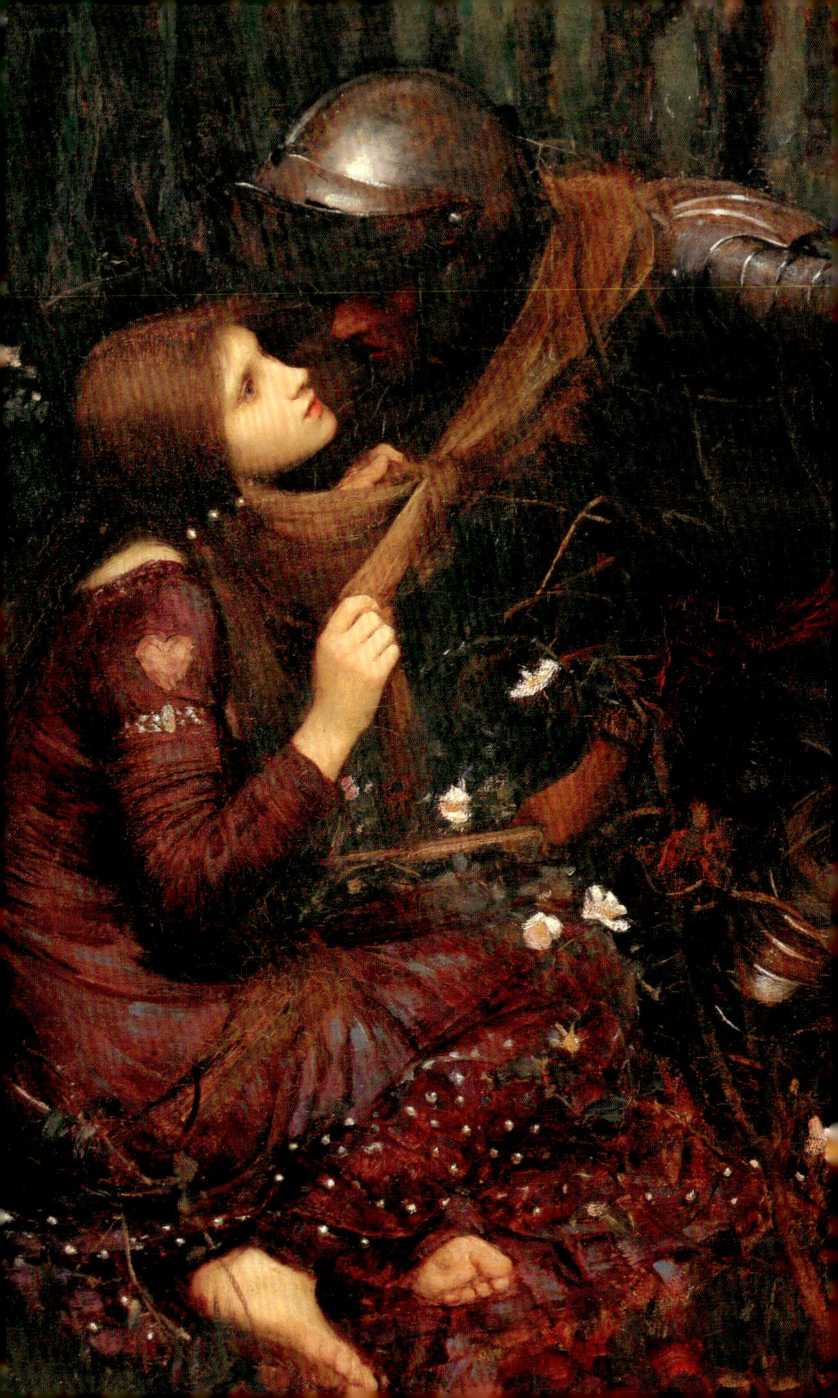

La Belle Dame sans Merci

John Keats

'O what can ail thee, knight-at-arms,
Alone and palely loitering?
The sedge is withered from the lake,
And no birds sing.

'O what can ail thee, knight-at-arms,
So haggard and so woe-begone?
The squirrel's granary is full,
And the harvest's done.

'I see a lily on thy brow,
With anguish moist and fever dew;
And on thy cheeks a fading rose
Fast withereth too.'

'I met a lady in the meads,
Full beautiful—a faery's child,
Her hair was long, her foot was light,
And her eyes were wild.

'I made a garland for her head,
And bracelets too, and fragrant zone;
She looked at me as she did love,
And made sweet moan.

'I set her on my pacing steed
And nothing else saw all day long,
For sidelong would she bend, and sing
A faery's song.

'She found me roots of relish sweet,
 And honey wild, and manna dew,
And sure in language strange she said,—
 "I love thee true."

'She took me to her elfin grot,
 And there she wept and sighed full sore,
And there I shut her wild wild eyes
 With kisses four.

'And there she lullèd me asleep,
 And there I dreamed—Ah! woe betide!
The latest dream I ever dreamed
 On the cold hill's side.

'I saw pale kings and princes too,
 Pale warriors, death-pale were they all;
They cried—"La belle Dame sans Merci
 Hath thee in thrall!"

'I saw their starved lips in the gloam,
 With horrid warning gapèd wide,
And I awoke and found me here,
 On the cold hill's side.

'And this is why I sojourn here
 Alone and palely loitering,
Though the sedge is withered from the lake,
 And no birds sing.'

from

~ MAUD ~

ALFRED TENNYSON

I have led her home, my love, my only friend.
There is none like her, none.
And never yet so warmly ran my blood
And sweetly, on and on
Calming itself to the long-wished-for end,
Full to the banks, close on the promised good.

None like her, none.
Just now the dry-tongued laurels' pattering talk
Seemed her light foot along the garden walk,
And shook my heart to think she comes once more;
But even then I heard her close the door,
The gates of Heaven are closed, and she is gone.

There is none like her, none.
Nor will be when our summers have deceased.
O, art thou sighing for Lebanon
In the long breeze that streams to thy delicious East,
Sighing for Lebanon,
Dark cedar, tho' thy limbs have here increased,
Upon a pastoral slope as fair,

And looking to the South, and fed
With honeyed rain and delicate air,
And haunted by the starry head
Of her whose gentle will has changed my fate,
And made my life a perfumed altar-flame;
And over whom thy darkness must have spread
With such delights as theirs of old, thy great
Forefathers of the thornless garden, there
Shadowing the snow-limbed Eve from whom she came.

Here will I lie, while these long branches sway,
And you fair stars that crown a happy day
Go in and out as if at merry play,
Who am no more so all forlorn,
As when it seemed far better to be born
To labour and the mattock-hardened hand,
Than nursed at ease and brought to understand
A sad astrology, the boundless plan
That makes you tyrants in your iron skies,
Innumerable, pitiless, passionless eyes,
Cold fires, yet with the power to burn and brand
His nothingness into man.

But now shine on, and what care I,
Who in this stormy gulf have found a pearl
The countercharm of space and hollow sky,
And do accept my madness, and would die
To save from some slight shame one simple girl.

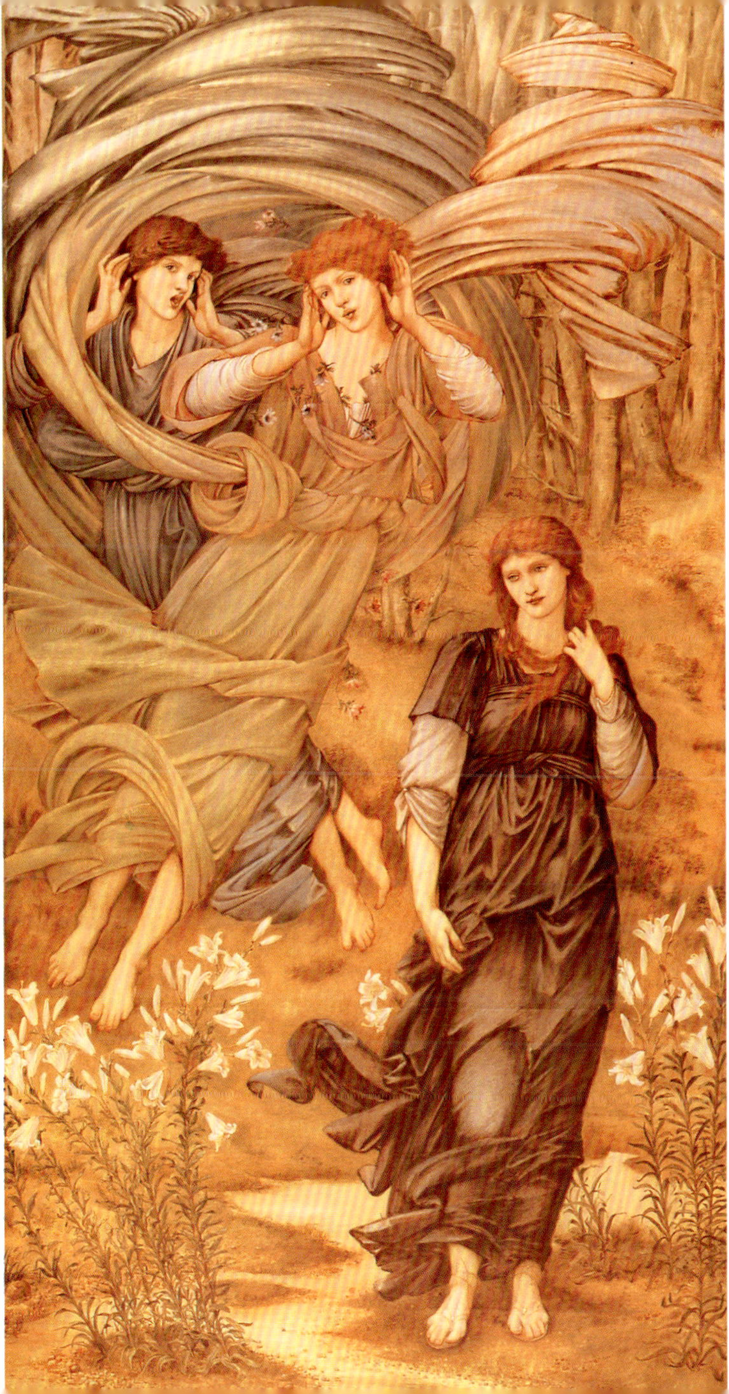

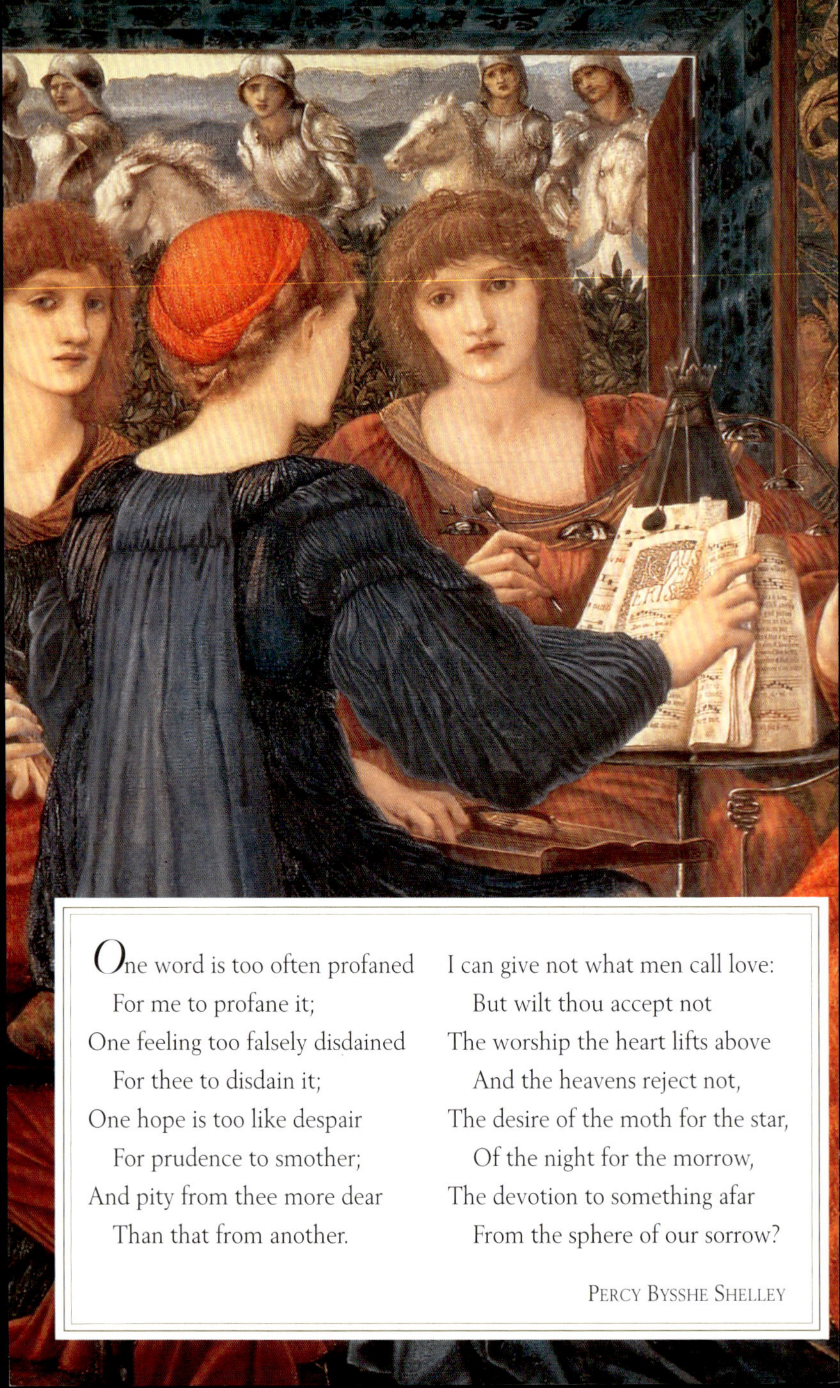

One word is too often profaned
For me to profane it;
One feeling too falsely disdained
For thee to disdain it;
One hope is too like despair
For prudence to smother;
And pity from thee more dear
Than that from another.

I can give not what men call love:
But wilt thou accept not
The worship the heart lifts above
And the heavens reject not,
The desire of the moth for the star,
Of the night for the morrow,
The devotion to something afar
From the sphere of our sorrow?

PERCY BYSSHE SHELLEY

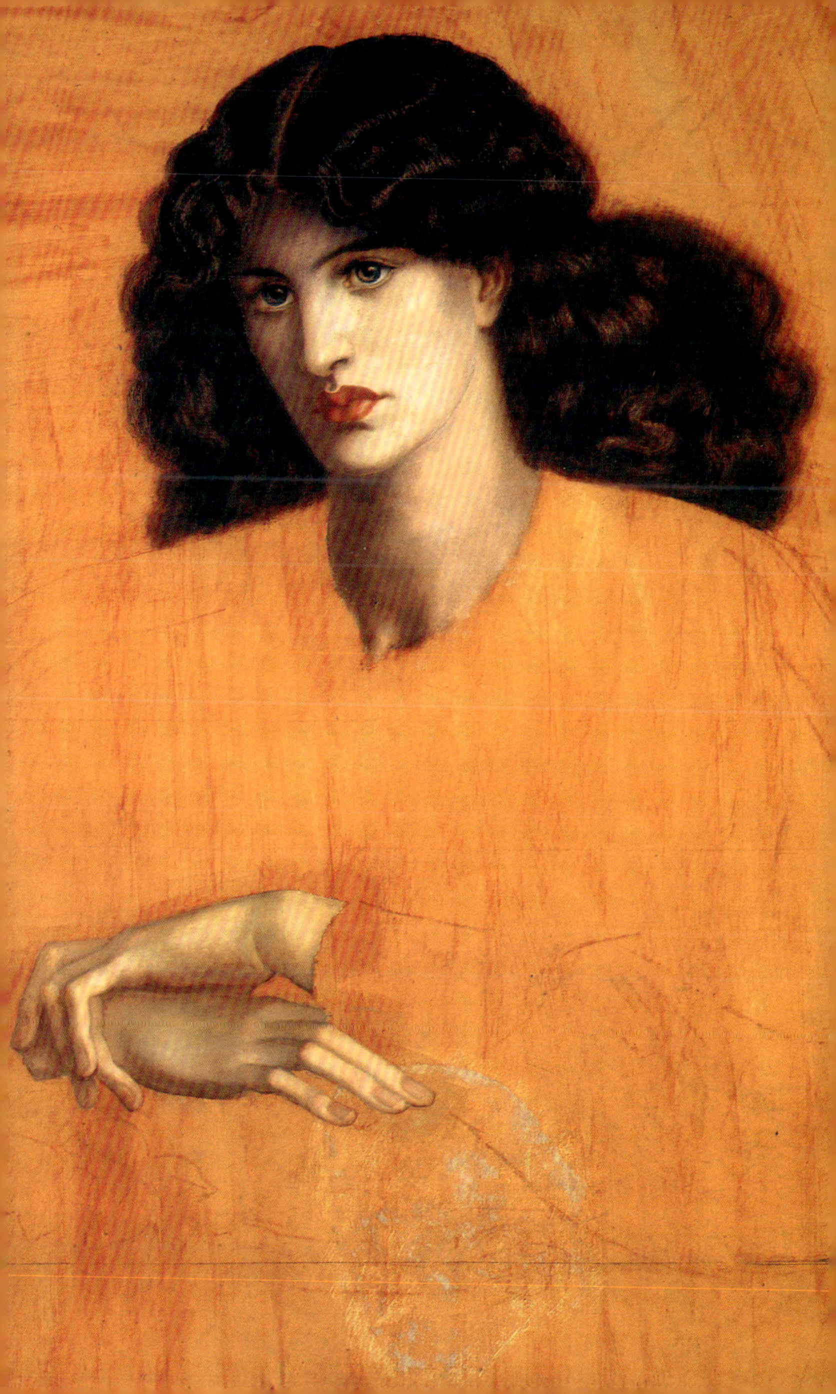

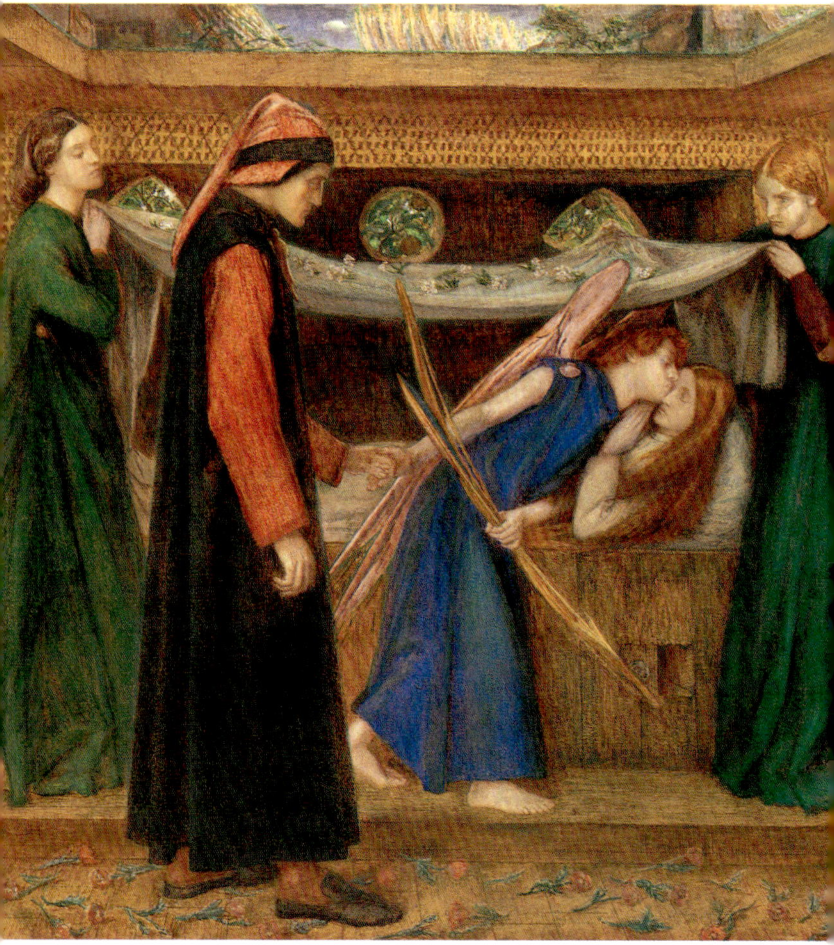

Dante's Dream

Dante Gabriel Rossetti

The sun ceased and the stars began to gather,
And each wept at the other;
And birds dropped at midflight out of the sky
And earth shook suddenly:
And I was 'ware of one, hoarse and tired out,
Who asked of me 'Hast thou not heard it said
The lady, she that was so fair, is dead?'
Then lifting up mine eyes, as the tears came,
I saw the angels like a rain of Manna
In a long flight flying back Heavenwards,
Having a little cloud in front of them,
After which they went and said 'Hosanna',
And if they had said more you should have heard.
Then Love spoke thus: 'Now all shall be made clear,
Come and behold our lady where she lies.'
These idle Phantasies
Then carried me to see my lady dead,
And standing at her head
Her ladies put a white veil over her;
And with her was such very humbleness
That she appeared to say 'I am at peace.'

from

~ Mariana ~

Alfred Tennyson

With blackest moss the flower-plots
  Were thickly crusted, one and all:
The rusted nails fell from the knots
  That held the pear to the gable-wall.
The broken sheds look'd sad and strange:
  Unlifted was the clinking latch;
  Weeded and worn the ancient thatch
Upon the lonely moated grange.
    She only said, 'My life is dreary,
      He cometh not,' she said;
    She said, 'I am aweary, aweary,
      I would that I were dead!'

The sparrow's chirrup on the roof,
  The slow clock ticking, and the sound
Which to the wooing wind aloof
  The poplar made, did all confound
Her sense; but most she loathed the hour
  When the thick-moted sunbeam lay
  Athwart the chambers, and the day
Was sloping toward his western bower.
    Then, said she, 'I am very dreary,
      He will not come,' she said;
    She wept, 'I am aweary, aweary,
      Oh God, that I were dead!'

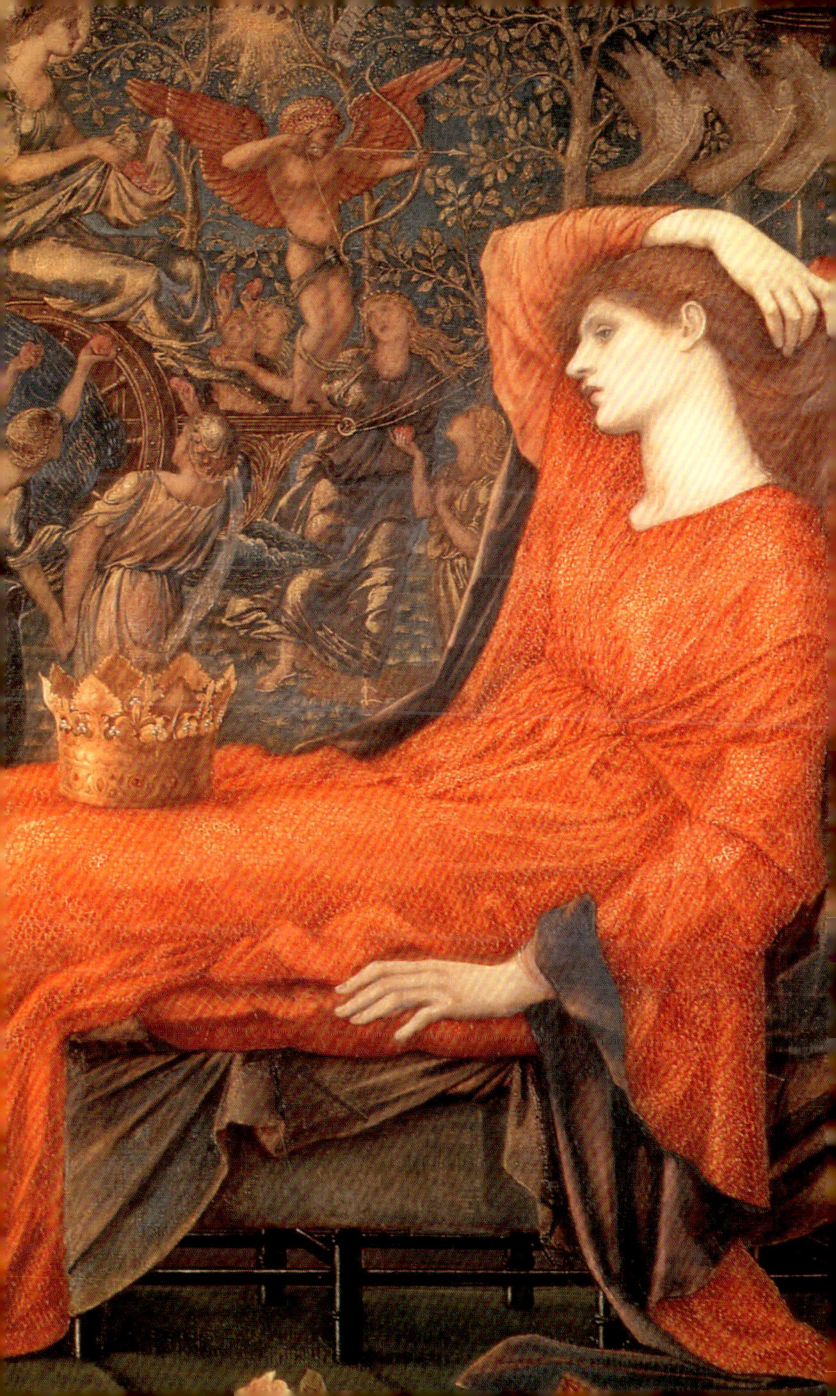

THE FLIGHT OF LOVE

PERCY BYSSHE SHELLEY

When the lamp is shattered
The light in the dust lies dead—
When the cloud is scattered,
The rainbow's glory is shed.
When the lute is broken,
Sweet tones are remembered not;
When the lips have spoken,
Loved accents are soon forgot.

As music and splendour
Survive not the lamp nor the lute,
The heart's echoes render
No song when the spirit is mute—
No song but sad dirges,
Like the wind through a ruined cell,
Or the mournful surges
That ring the dead seaman's knell.

When hearts have once mingled,
Love first leaves the well-built nest;
The weak one is singled
To endure what it once possessed.
O Love! who bewailest
The frailty of all things here,
Why choose you the frailest
For your cradle, your home, and your bier?

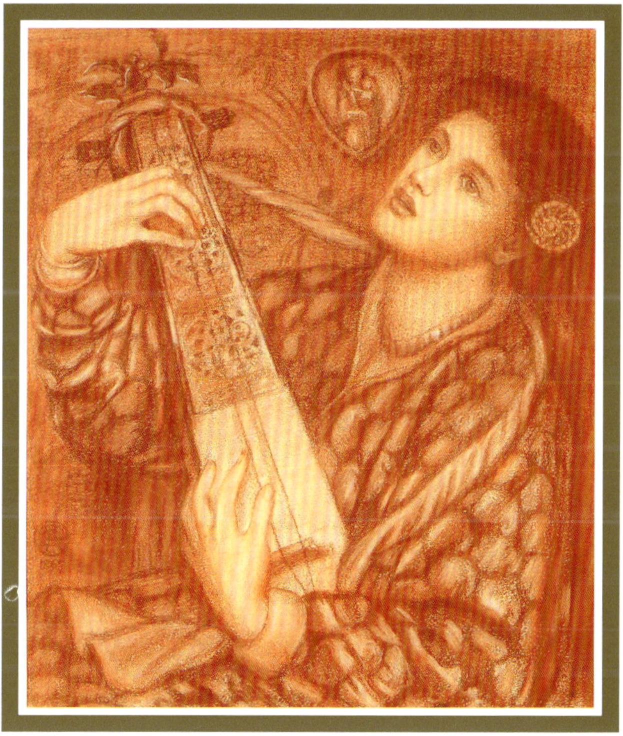

Its passions will rock thee
As the storms rock the ravens on high;
Bright reason will mock thee
Like the sun from a wintry sky.
From thy nest every rafter
Will rot, and thine eagle home
Leave thee naked to laughter,
When leaves fall and cold winds come.

from

La Vita Nuova

Dante Alighieri

translated by Dante Gabriel Rossetti

Mine eyes beheld the blessed pity spring
  Into thy countenance immediately
  A while agone, when thou beheldst in me
The sickness only hidden grief can bring;
And then I knew thou wast considering
  How abject and forlorn my life must be;
  And I became afraid that thou shouldst see
My weeping, and account it a base thing.
Therefore I went out from thee; feeling how
  The tears were straightway loosened at my heart
  Beneath thine eyes' compassionate control;
  And afterwards I said within my soul:
  'Lo! with this lady dwells the counterpart
Of the same Love who holds me weeping now.'

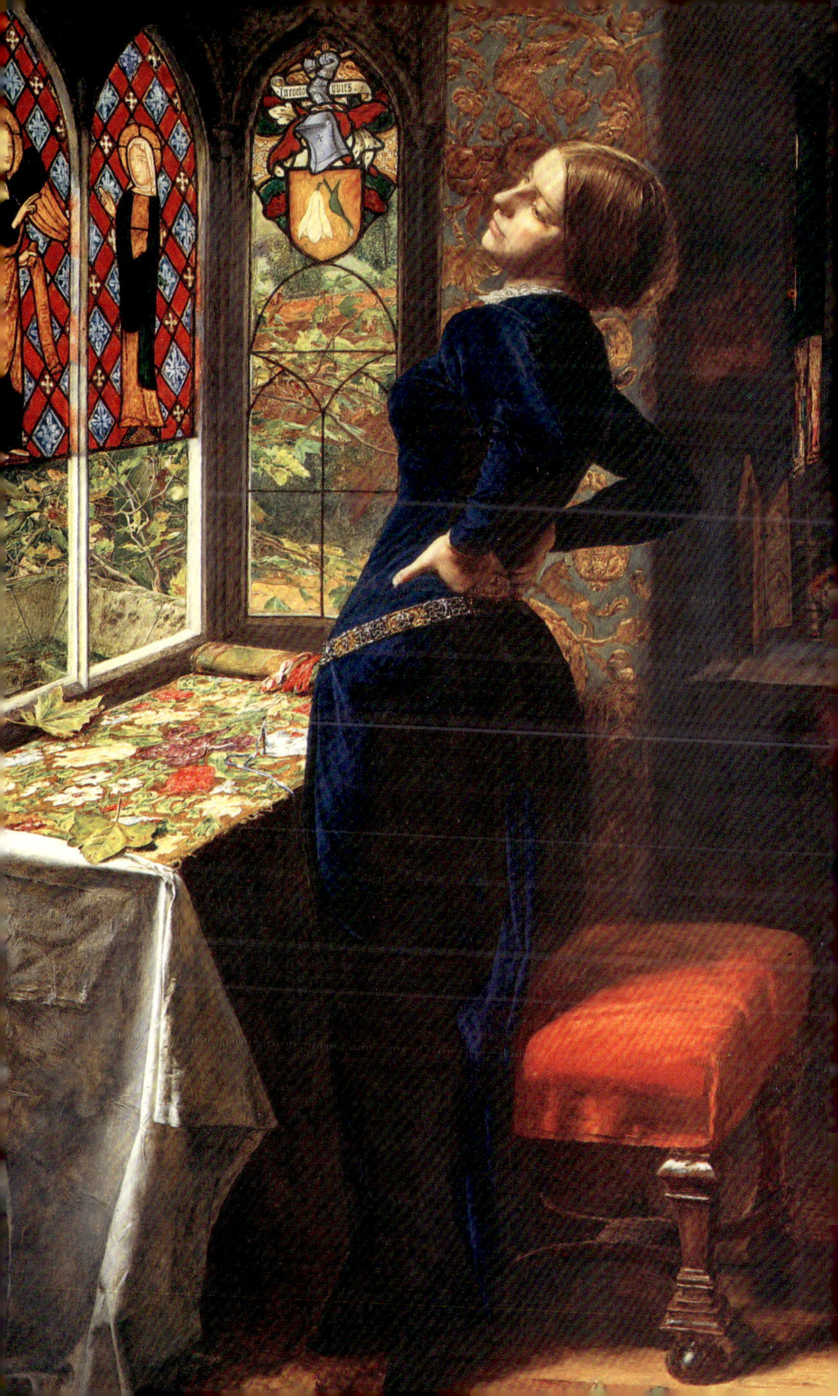

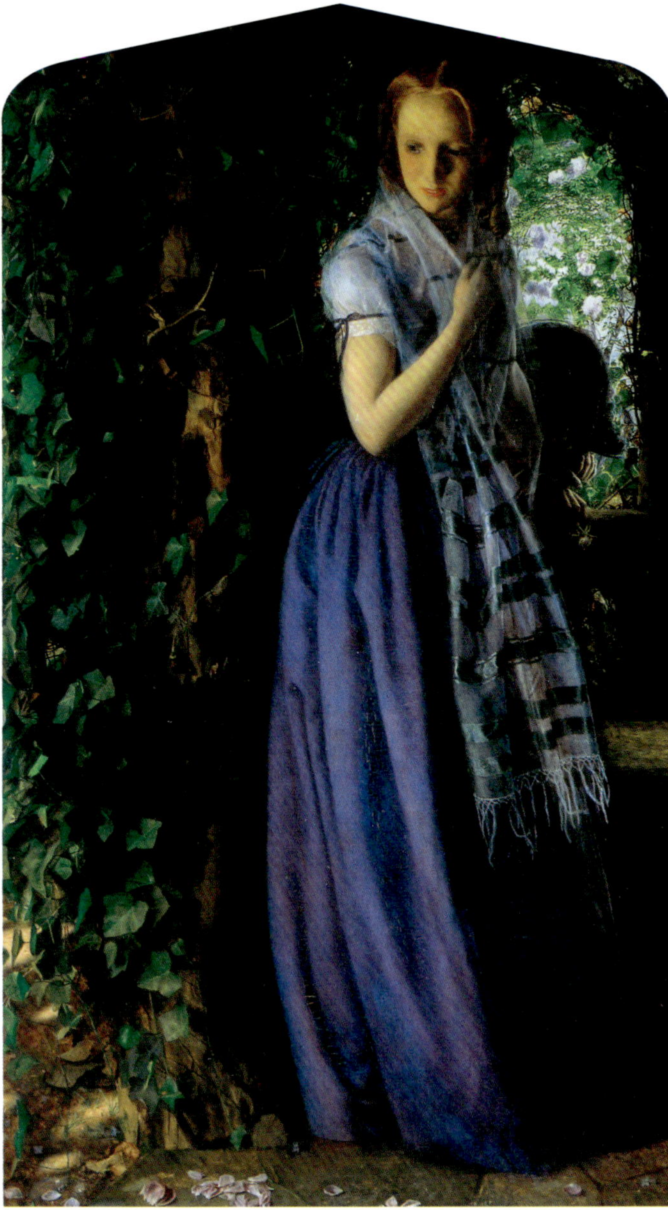

from

~ THE MILLER'S DAUGHTER ~

ALFRED TENNYSON

Love that hath us in the net,
Can we pass, and we forget?
Many suns arise and set.
Many a chance the years beget.
Love the gift is Love the debt.
Even so.
Love is hurt with jar and fret.
Love is made a vague regret.
Eyes with idle tears are wet.
Idle habit links us yet.
What is love? for we forget:
Ah, no! no!

from

Praise of My Lady

William Morris

My lady seems of ivory
Forehead, straight nose, and cheeks that be
Hollowed a little mournfully.
Beata mea Domina!

Her forehead, overshadowed much
By bows of hair, has a wave such
As God was good to make for me.
Beata mea Domina!

Not greatly long my lady's hair,
Nor yet with yellow colour fair,
But thick and crispèd wonderfully:
Beata mea Domina!

Heavy to make the pale face sad,
And dark, but dead as though it had
Been forged by God most wonderfully
—Beata mea Domina!—

Of some strange metal, thread by thread,
To stand out from my lady's head,
Not moving much to tangle me.
Beata mea Domina!

Beneath her brows the lids fall slow,
The lashes a clear shadow throw
Where I would wish my lips to be.
Beata mea Domina!

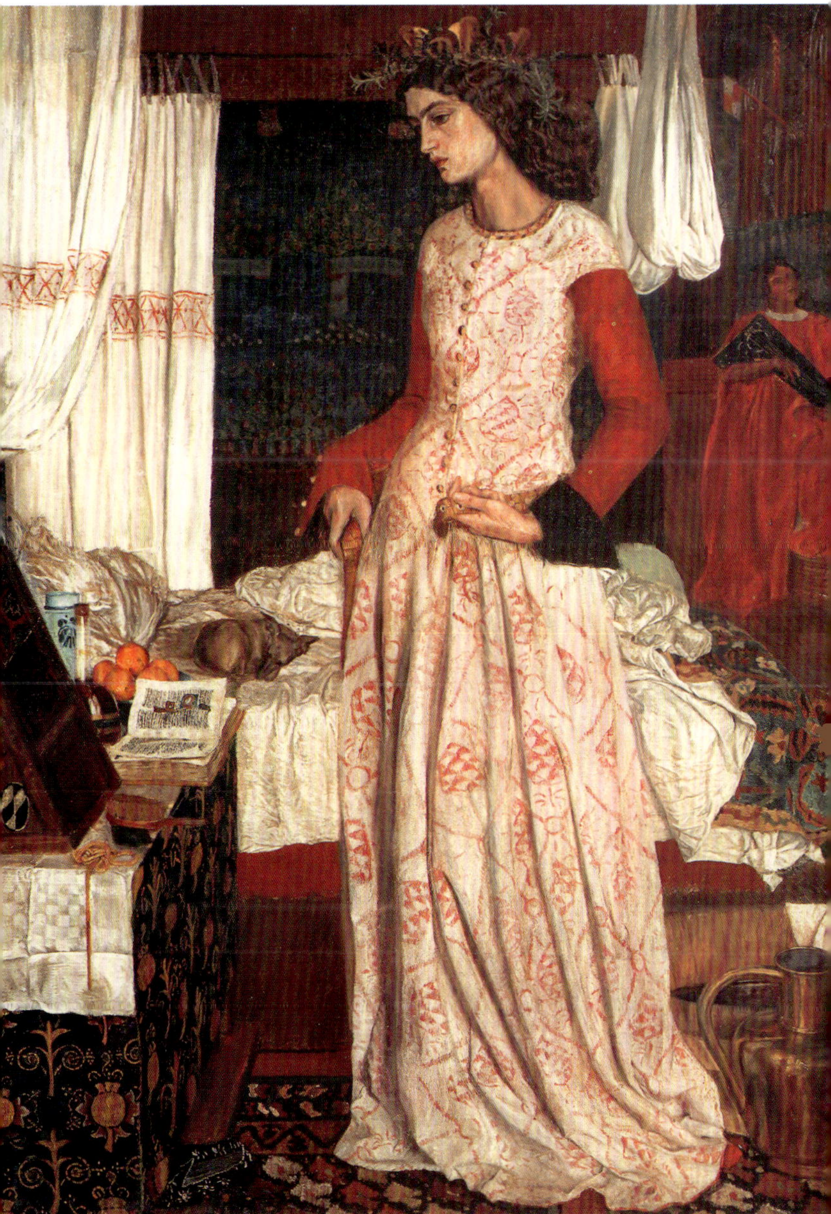

None of Beauty's Daughters

George Gordon Byron

There be none of Beauty's daughters
With a magic like Thee;
And like music on the waters
Is thy sweet voice to me:
When, as if its sound were causing
The charmèd ocean's pausing,
The waves lie still and gleaming,
And the lulled winds seem dreaming:

And the midnight moon is weaving
Her bright chain o'er the deep,
Whose breast is gently heaving
As an infant's asleep:
So the spirit bows before thee
To listen and adore thee;
With a full but soft emotion,
Like the swell of Summer's ocean.

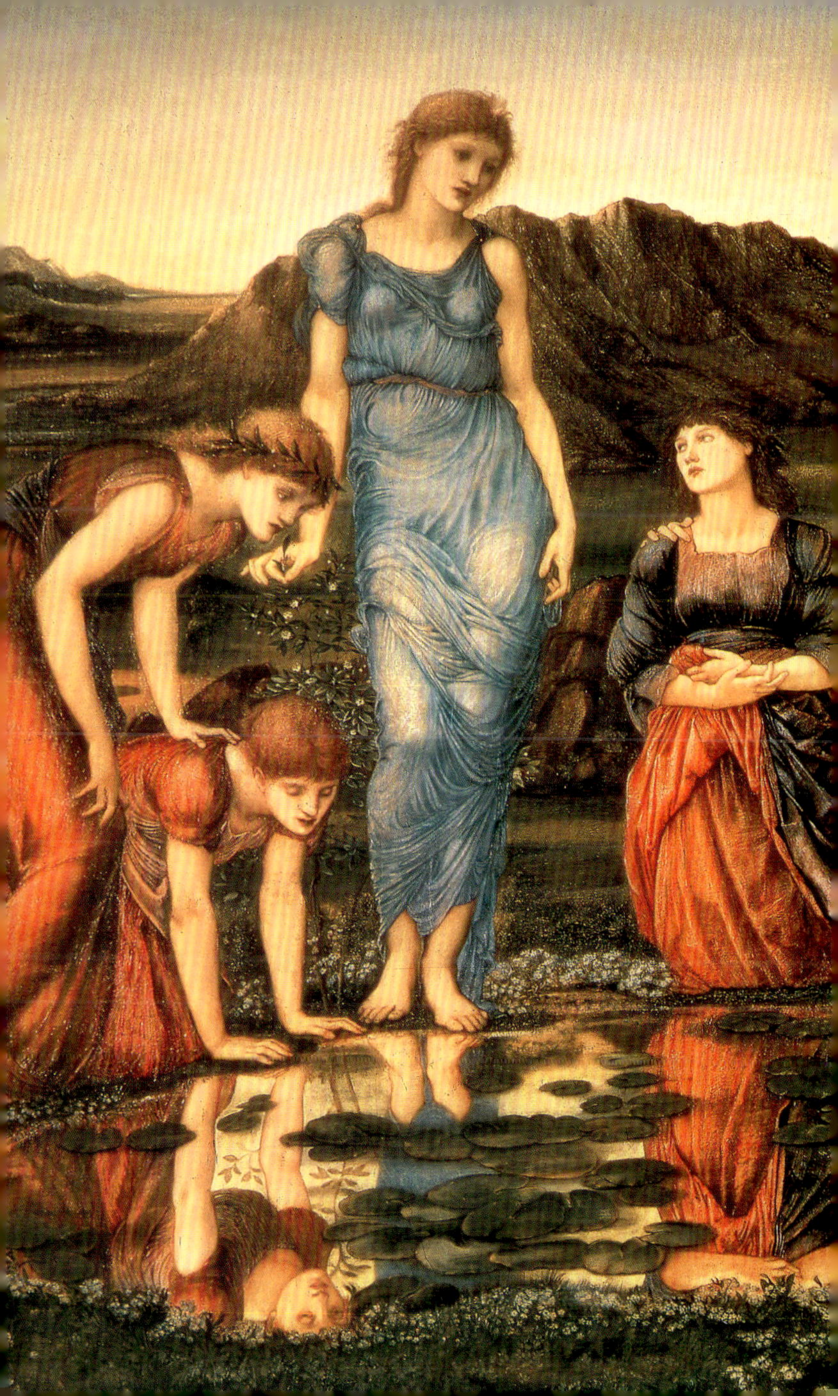

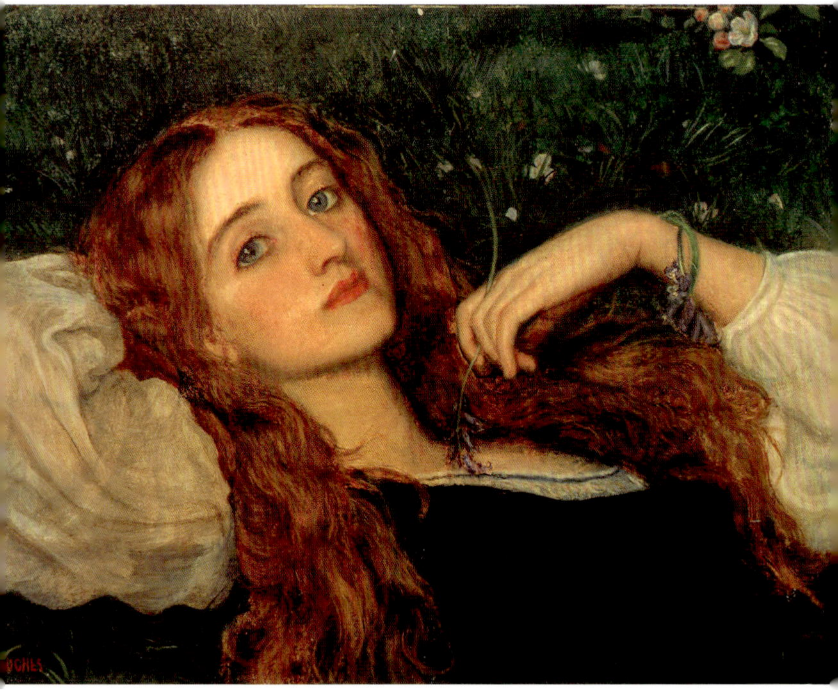

To One in Paradise

Edgar Allan Poe

Thou wast all that to me, love,
  For which my soul did pine—
A green isle in the sea, love,
  A fountain and a shrine,
All wreathed with fairy fruits and flowers,
  And all the flowers were mine.

Now all my days are trances,
  And all my nightly dreams
Are where thy grey eye glances,
  And where thy footstep gleams—
In what ethereal dances,
  By what eternal streams!

The Blessèd Damozel

Dante Gabriel Rossetti

The blessèd damozel leaned out
  From the gold bar of Heaven;
Her eyes were deeper than the depth
  Of waters stilled at even;
She had three lilies in her hand,
  And the stars in her hair were seven.

Her robe, ungirt from clasp to hem,
  No wrought flowers did adorn,
But a white rose of Mary's gift,
  For service meetly worn;
Her hair that lay along her back
  Was yellow like ripe corn.

Herseemed she scarce had been a day
  One of God's choristers;
The wonder was not yet quite gone
  From that still look of hers;
Albeit, to them she left, her day
  Had counted as ten years.

(To one, it is ten years of years.
  . . . Yet now, and in this place,
Surely she leaned o'er me—her hair
  Fell all about my face. . .
Nothing: the autumn-fall of leaves.
  The whole year sets apace.)

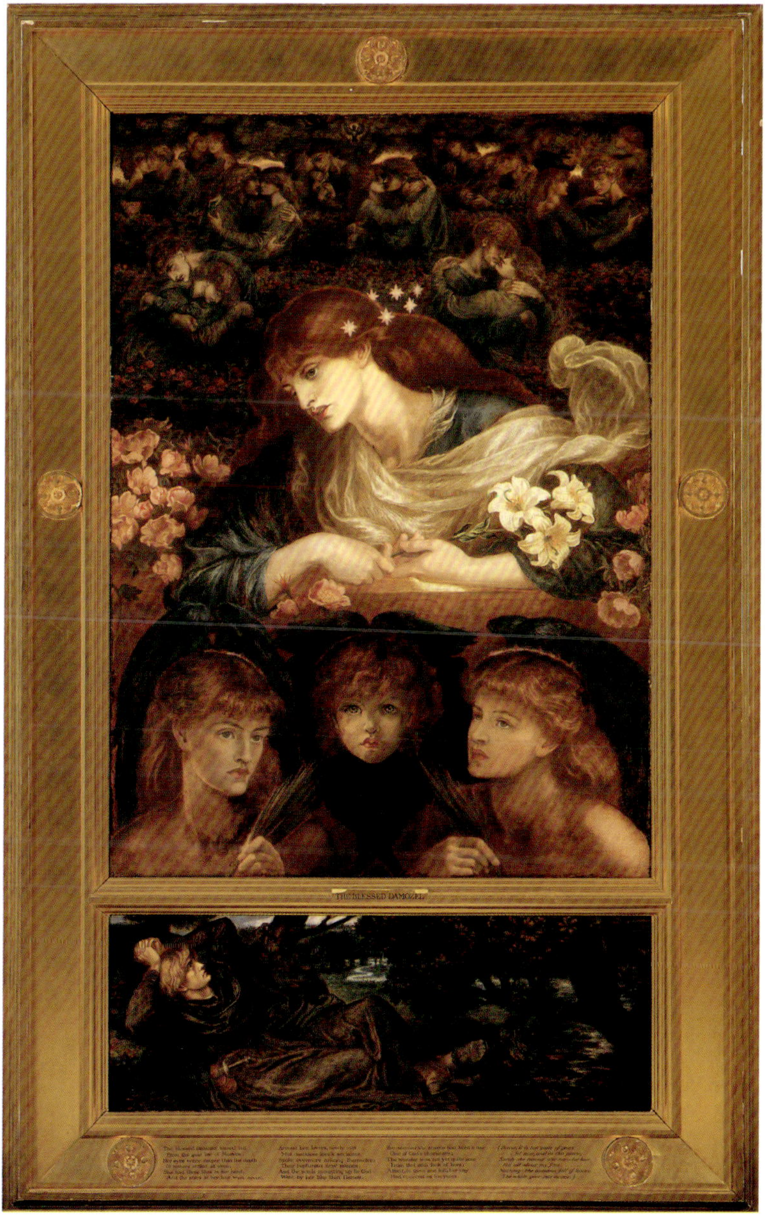
THE BLESSED DAMOZEL

It was the rampart of God's house
 That she was standing on;
By God built over the sheer depth
 The which is Space begun;
So high, that looking downward thence
 She scarce could see the sun.

It lies in Heaven, across the flood
 Of ether, as a bridge.
Beneath, the tides of day and night
 With flame and darkness ridge
The void, as low as where this earth
 Spins like a fretful midge.

Around her, lovers, newly met
 'Mid deathless love's acclaims,
Spoke evermore among themselves
 Their heart-remembered names;
And the souls mounting up to God
 Went by her like thin flames.

And still she bowed herself and stooped
 Out of the circling charm;
Until her bosom must have made
 The bar she leaned on warm,
And the lilies lay as if asleep
 Along her bended arm.

From the fixed place of Heaven she saw
   Time like a pulse shake fierce
Through all the worlds. Her gaze still strove
   Within the gulf to pierce
Its path; and now she spoke as when
   The stars sang in their spheres.

The sun was gone now; the curled moon
   Was like a little feather
Fluttering far down the gulf; and now
   She spoke through the still weather.
Her voice was like the voice the stars
   Had when they sang together.

(Ah sweet! Even now, in that bird's song,
   Strove not her accents there,
Fain to be hearkened? When those bells
   Possessed the mid-day air,
Strove not her steps to reach my side
   Down all the echoing stair?)

'I wish that he were come to me,
   For he will come,' she said.
'Have I not prayed in Heaven?—on earth,
   Lord, Lord, has he not prayed?
Are not two prayers a perfect strength?
   And shall I feel afraid?

'When round his head the aureole clings,
And he is clothed in white,
I'll take his hand and go with him
To the deep wells of light;
As unto a stream we will step down,
And bathe there in God's sight.

'We two will stand beside that shrine,
Occult, withheld, untrod,
Whose lamps are stirred continually
With prayer sent up to God;
And see our old prayers, granted, melt
Each like a little cloud.

'We two will lie i' the shadow of
That living mystic tree
Within whose secret growth the Dove
Is sometimes felt to be,
While every leaf that His plumes touch
Saith His Name audibly.

'And I myself will teach to him,
I myself, lying so,
The songs I sing here; which his voice
Shall pause in, hushed and slow,
And find some knowledge at each pause,
Or some new thing to know.'

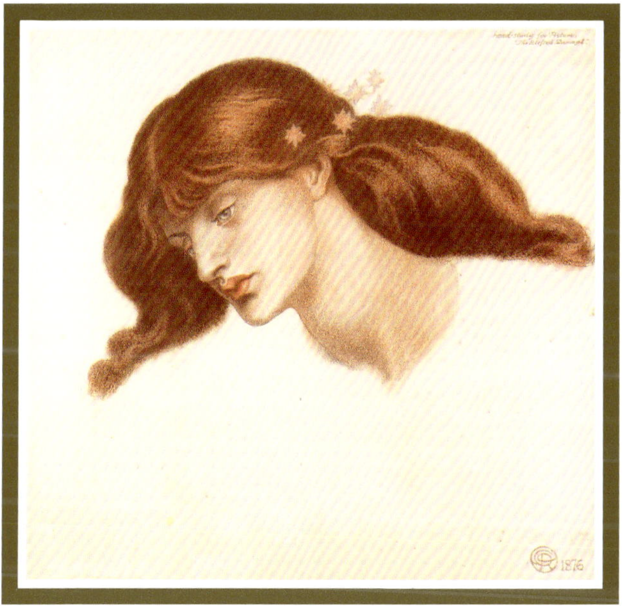

(Alas! we two, we two, thou say'st!
  Yea, one wast thou with me
That once of old. But shall God lift
  To endless unity
The soul whose likeness with thy soul
  Was but its love for thee?)

'We two,' she said, 'will seek the groves
  Where the lady Mary is,
With her five handmaidens, whose names
  Are five sweet symphonies,
Cecily, Gertrude, Magdalen,
  Margaret and Rosalys.

'Circlewise sit they, with bound locks
   And foreheads garlanded;
Into the fine cloth white like flame
   Weaving the golden thread,
To fashion the birth-robes for them
   Who are just born, being dead.

'He shall fear, haply, and be dumb:
   Then will I lay my cheek
To his, and tell about our love,
   Not once abashed or weak:
And the dear Mother will approve
   My pride, and let me speak.

'Herself shall bring us, hand in hand,
   To Him round whom all souls
Kneel, the clear-ranged unnumbered heads
   Bowed with their aureoles:
And angels meeting us shall sing
   To their citherns and citoles.

'There will I ask of Christ the Lord
   Thus much for him and me:—
Only to live as once on earth
   With Love,—only to be,
As then awhile, for ever now
   Together, I and he.'

She gazed and listened and then said,
  Less sad of speech than mild,—
'All this is when he comes.' She ceased.
  The light thrilled towards her, fill'd
With angels in strong level flight.
  Her eyes prayed, and she smil'd.

(I saw her smile.) But soon their path
  Was vague in distant spheres:
And then she cast her arms along
  The golden barriers,
And laid her face between her hands,
  And wept. (I heard her tears.)

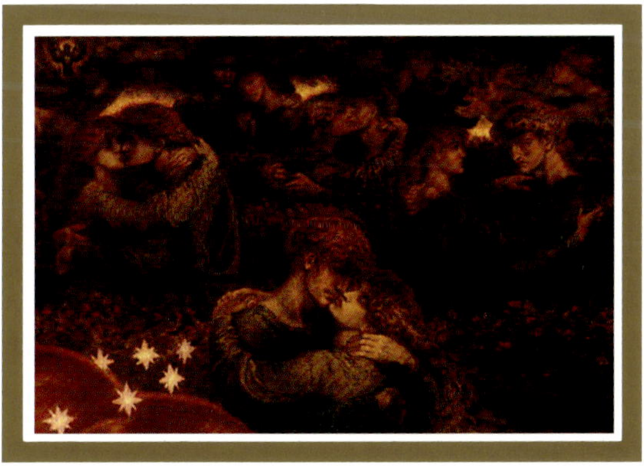

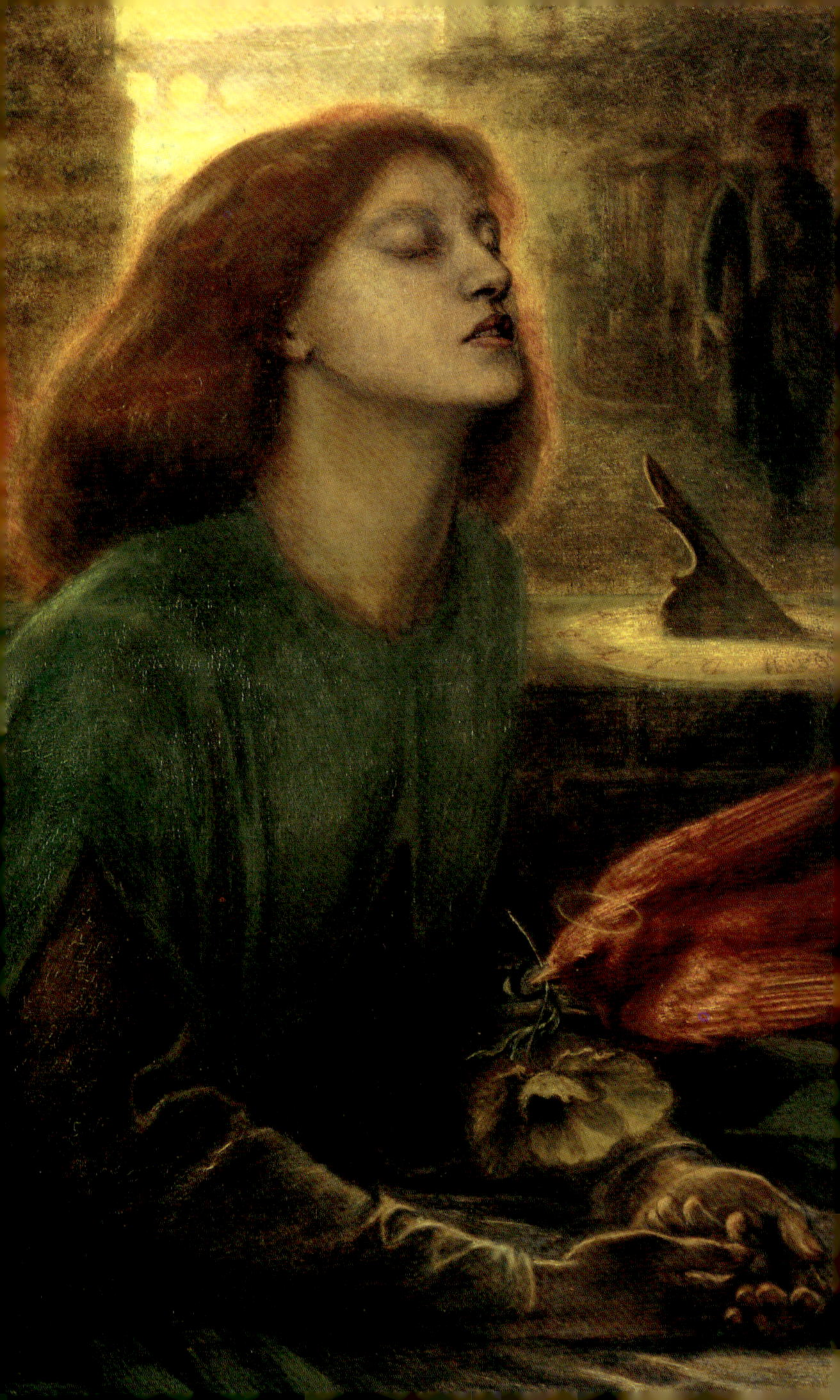

~ Rest ~

Christina Rossetti

O Earth, lie heavily upon her eyes;
Seal her sweet eyes weary of watching, Earth;
Lie close around her; leave no room for mirth
With its harsh laughter, nor for sound of sighs.
She hath no questions, she hath no replies,
Hushed in and curtained with a blessèd dearth
Of all that irked her from the hour of birth;
With stillness that is almost Paradise.
Darkness more clear than noonday holdeth her,
Silence more musical than any song;
Even her very heart has ceased to stir:
Until the morning of Eternity
Her rest shall not begin nor end, but be;
And when she wakes she will not think it long.

Venus Verticordia

Dante Gabriel Rossetti

She hath the apple in her hand for thee,
Yet almost in her heart would hold it back;
She muses, with her eyes upon the track
Of that which in thy spirit they can see.
Haply, 'Behold, he is at peace,' saith she;
'Alas! the apple for his lips,—the dart
That follows its brief sweetness to his heart,—
The wandering of his feet perpetually!'

A little space her glance is still and coy;
But if she give the fruit that works her spell,
Those eyes shall flame as for her Phrygian boy.
Then shall her bird's strained throat the woe foretell,
And her far seas moan as a single shell,
And through her dark grove strike the light of Troy.

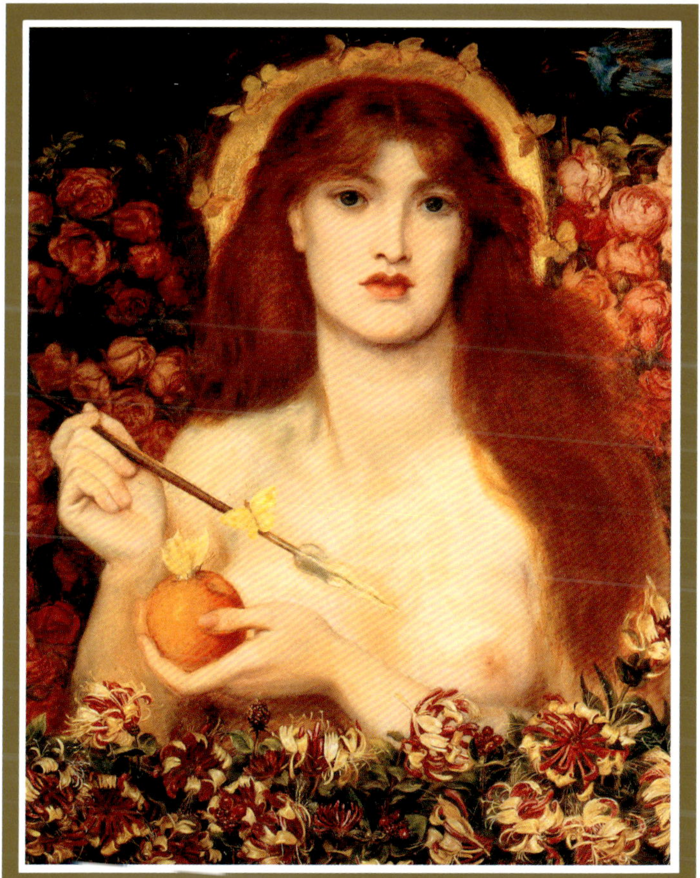

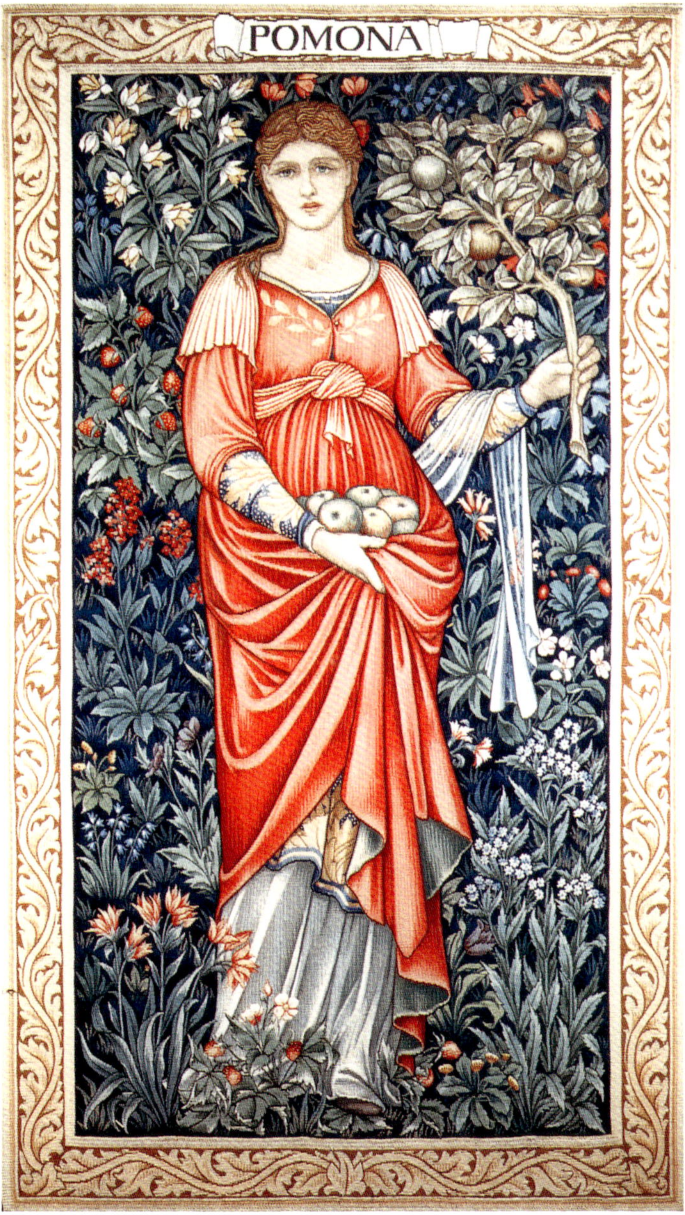
POMONA

A BIRTHDAY

CHRISTINA ROSSETTI

My heart is like a singing bird
   Whose nest is in a watered shoot;
My heart is like an apple tree
   Whose boughs are bent with thick-set fruit;
My heart is like a rainbow shell
   That paddles in a halcyon sea;
My heart is gladder than all these
   Because my love is come to me.

Raise me a dais of silk and down;
   Hang it with vair and purple dyes;
Carve it in doves and pomegranates,
   And peacocks with a hundred eyes;
Work it in gold and silver grapes,
   In leaves and silver fleurs-de-lys;
Because the birthday of my life
   Is come, my love is come to me.

Time of Roses

Thomas Hood

It was not in the Winter
   Our loving lot was cast;
It was the time of roses—
   We plucked them as we passed!

That churlish season never frowned
   On early lovers yet:
O no—the world was newly crowned
   With flowers when first we met!

'Twas twilight, and I bade you go,
   But still you held me fast;
It was the time of roses—
   We plucked them as we passed!

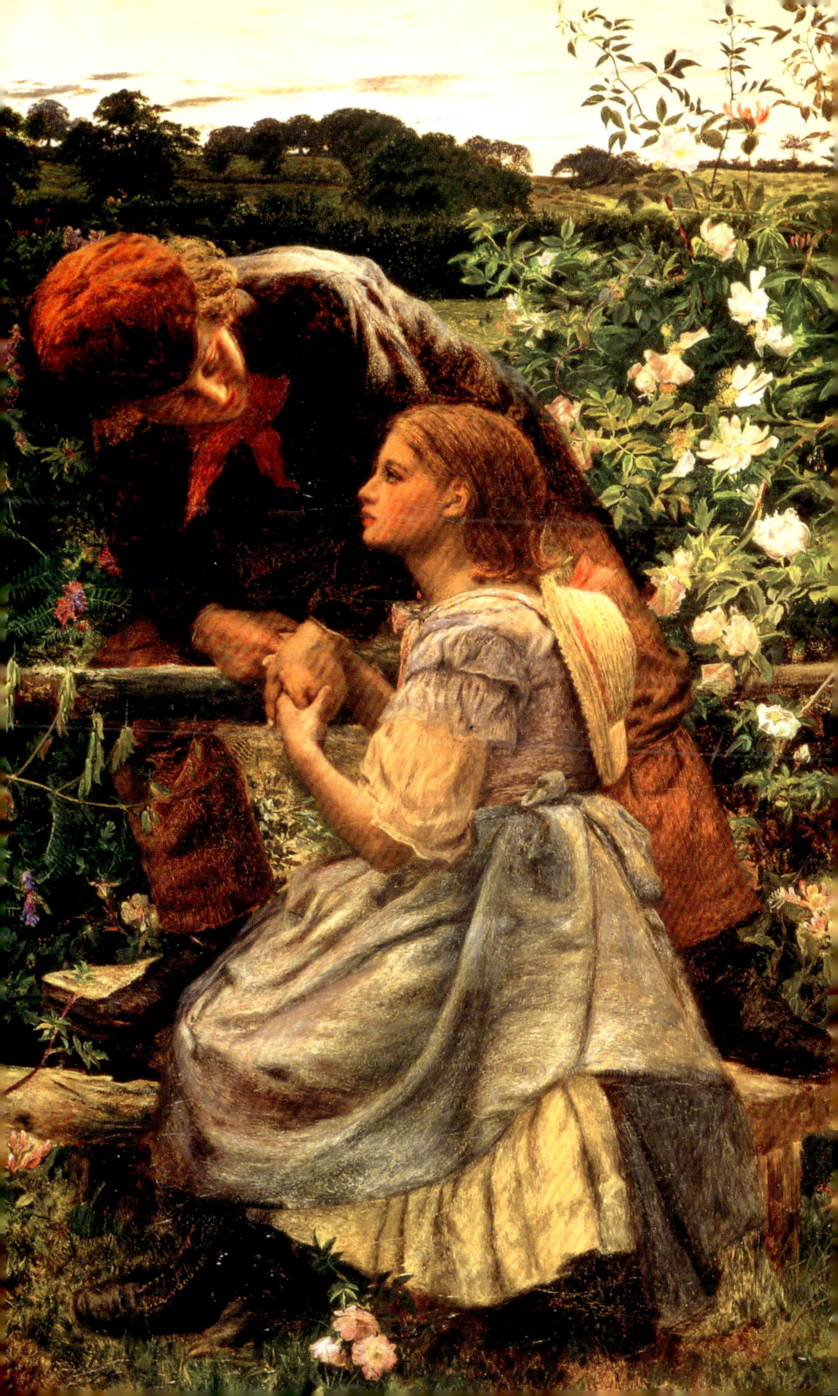

~ Proserpine ~

Dante Gabriel Rossetti

Afar away the light that brings cold cheer
   Unto this wall,—one instant and no more
   Admitted at my distant palace-door.
Afar the flowers of Enna from this drear
Dire fruit, which, tasted once, must thrall me here.
   Afar those skies from this Tartarean grey
   That chills me: and afar, how far away,
The nights that shall be from the days that were.

Afar from mine own self I seem, and wing
   Strange ways in thought, and listen for a sign:
   And still some heart unto some soul doth pine,
(Whose sounds mine inner sense is fain to bring,
Continually together murmuring)—
   "Woe's me for thee, unhappy Proserpine!"

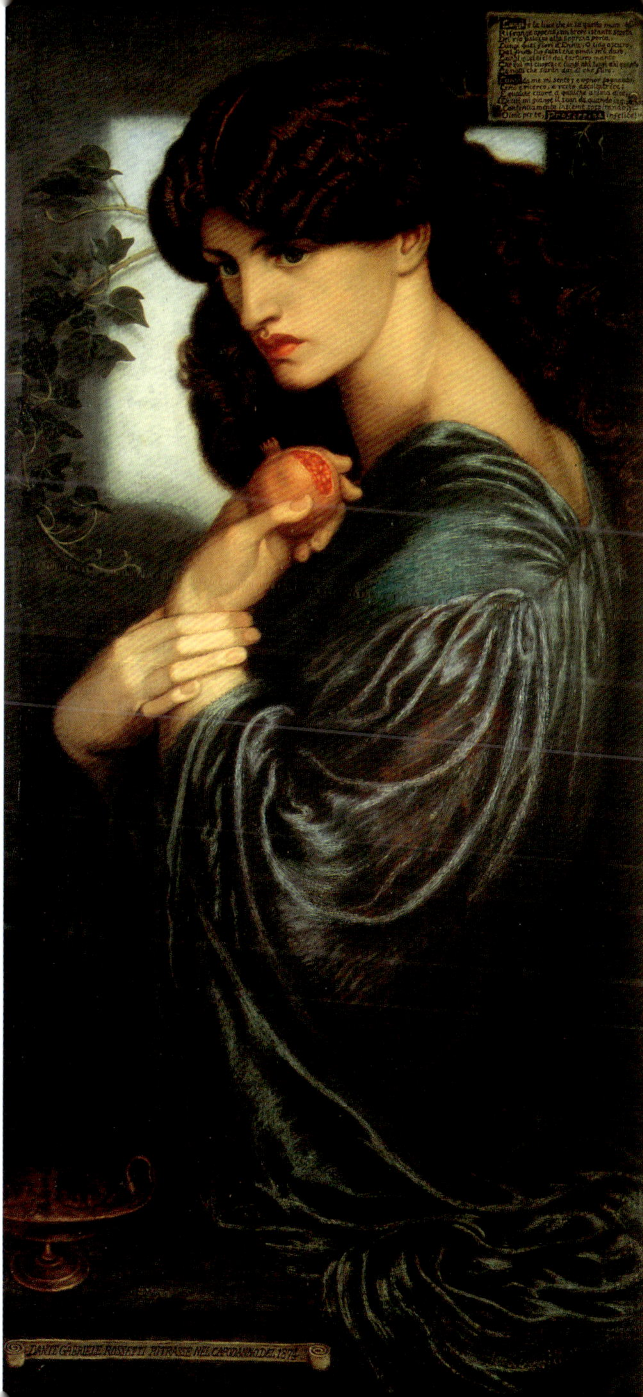

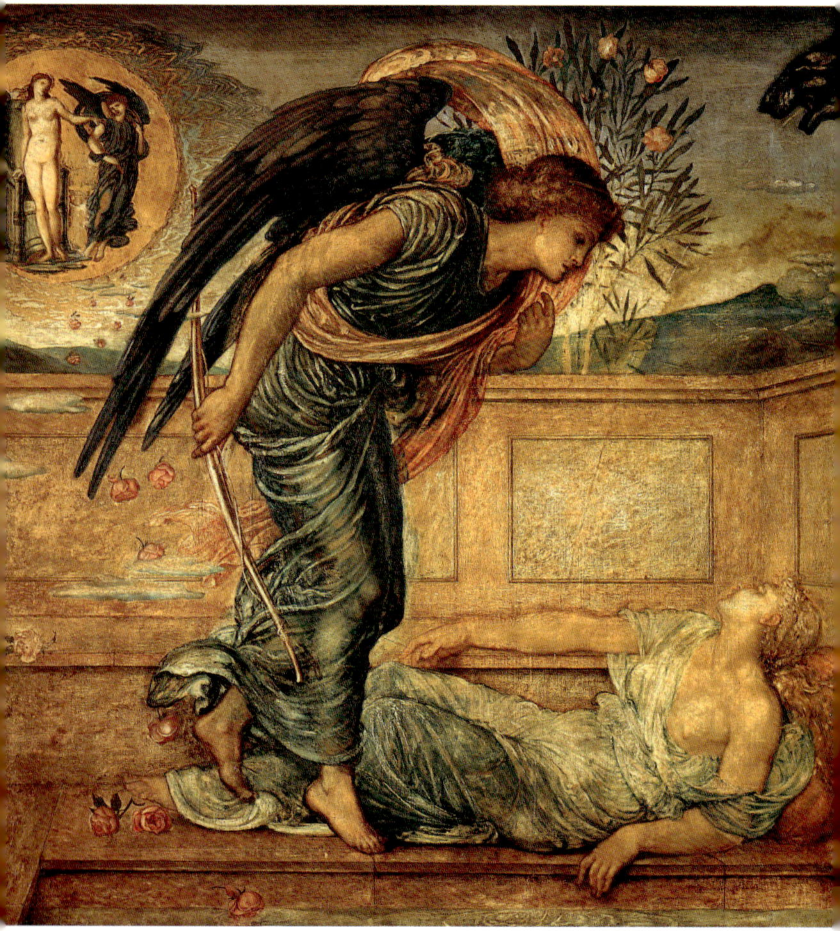

from

The Story of Cupid and Psyche

WILLIAM MORRIS

Within the flicker of a white-thorn shade
In gentle sleep he found the maiden laid.
One hand that held a book had fallen away
Across her body, and the other lay
Upon a marble fountain's plashing rim,
Among whose broken waves the fish showed dim,
But yet its wide-flung spray now woke her not,
Because the summer day at noon was hot,
And all sweet sounds and scents were lulling her.
So soon the rustle of his wings 'gan stir
Her looser folds of raiment, and the hair
Spread wide upon the grass and daisies fair,
As Love cast down his eyes with a half smile
Godlike and cruel; that faded in a while,
And long he stood above her hidden eyes
With red lips parted in a god's surprise.
Then very Love knelt down beside the maid
And on her breast a hand unfelt he laid,
And drew the gown from off her dainty feet,
And set his fair cheek to her shoulder sweet,
And kissed her lips that knew of no love yet,
And wondered if his heart would e'er forget
The perfect arm that o'er her body lay.

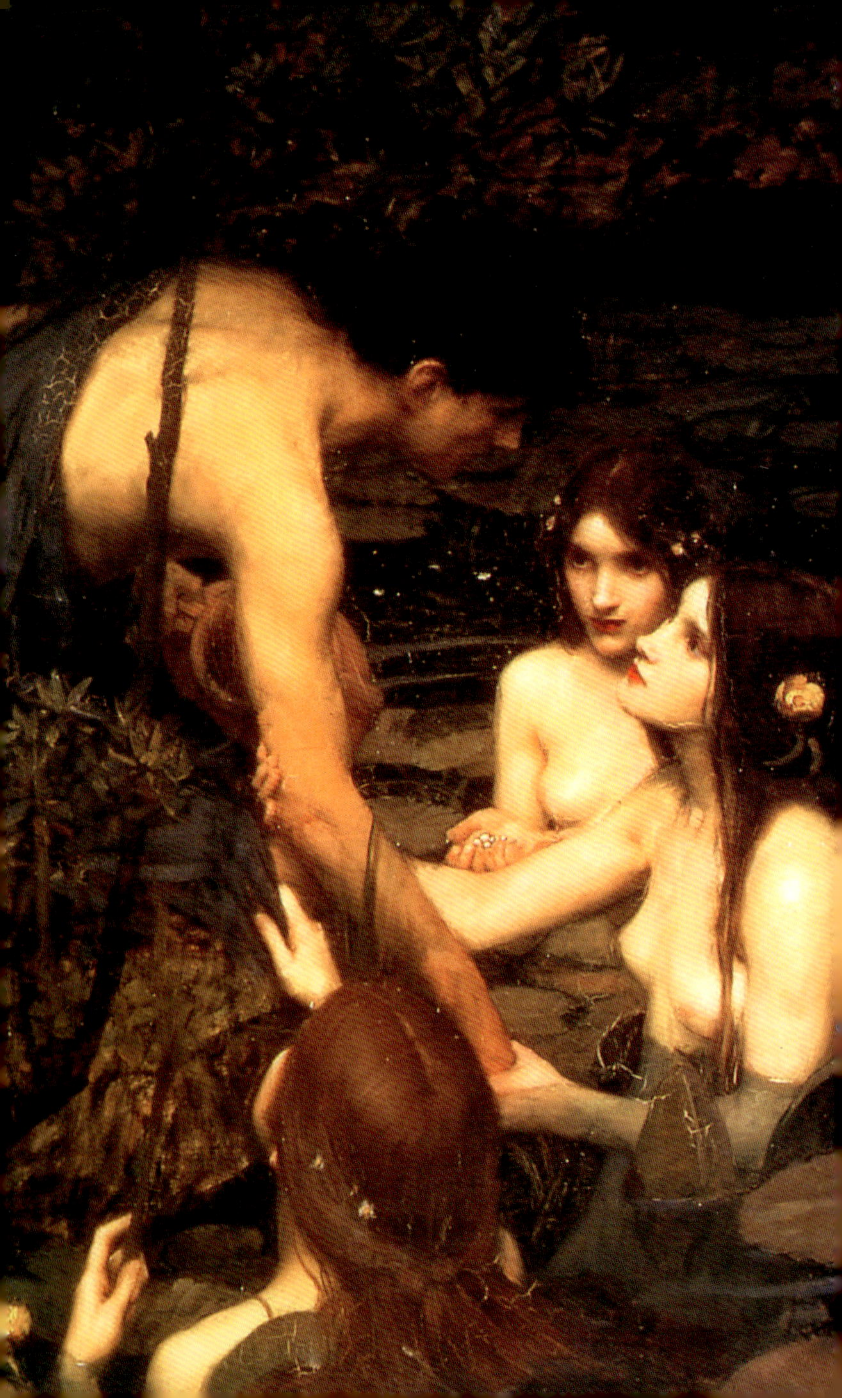

The Nymph's Song to Hylas

William Morris

I know a little garden-close
Set thick with lily and red rose,
Where I would wander if I might
From dewy dawn to dewy night,
And have one with me wandering.

And though within it no birds sing,
And though no pillared house is there,
And though the apple boughs are bare
Of fruit and blossom, would to God,
Her feet upon the green grass trod,
And I beheld them as before!

There comes a murmur from the shore,
And in the place two fair streams are,
Drawn from the purple hills afar,
Drawn down unto the restless sea;
The hills whose flowers ne'er fed the bee,
The shore no ship has ever seen,
Still beaten by the billows green,
Whose murmur comes unceasingly
Unto the place for which I cry.

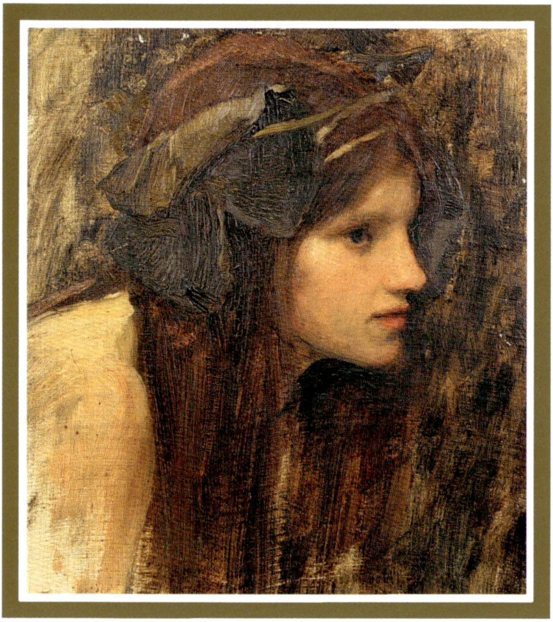

For which I cry both day and night,
For which I let slip all delight,
That maketh me both deaf and blind,
Careless to win, unskilled to find,
And quick to lose what all men seek.

Yet tottering as I am, and weak,
Still have I left a little breath
To seek within the jaws of death
An entrance to that happy place;
To seek the unforgotten face
Once seen, once kissed, once reft from me
Anigh the murmuring of the sea.

from

A Match

ALGERNON CHARLES SWINBURNE

If love were what the rose is,
And I were like the leaf,
Our lives would grow together
In sad or singing weather,
Blown fields or flowerful closes,
Green pleasure or grey grief;
If love were what the rose is,
And I were like the leaf.

If I were what the words are,
And love were like the tune,
With double sound and single
Delight our lips would mingle,
With kisses glad as birds are
That get sweet rain at noon;
If I were what the words are,
And love were like the tune.

If you were life, my darling,
And I your love were death,
We'd shine and snow together
Ere March made sweet the weather
With daffodil and starling
And hours of fruitful breath;
If you were life, my darling,
And I your love were death.

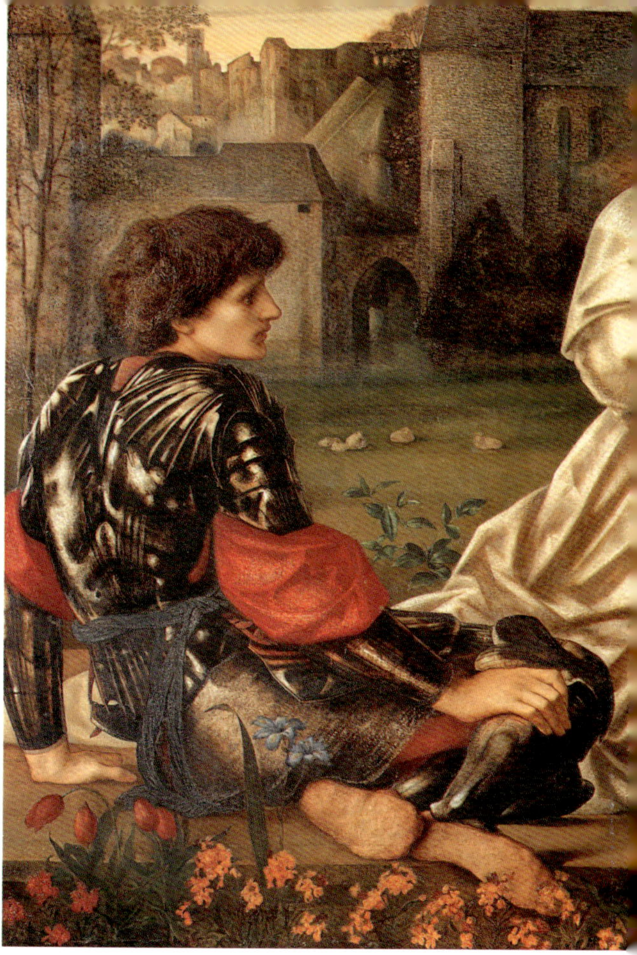

If you were April's lady,
   And I were lord in May,
We'd throw with leaves for hours
And draw for days with flowers,
Till day like night were shady,
   And night were bright like day;
If you were April's lady,
   And I were lord in May.

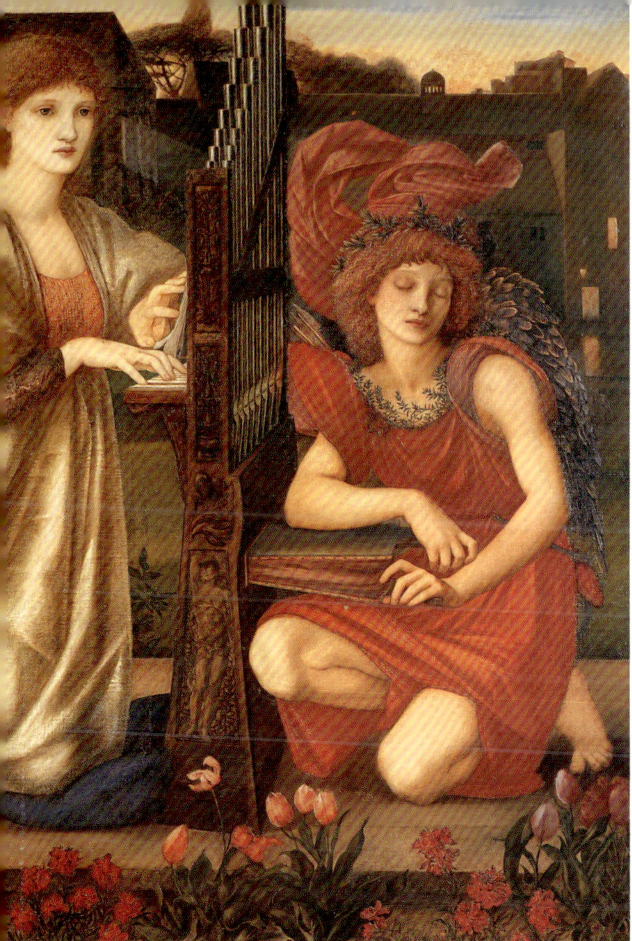

If you were queen of pleasure,
  And I were king of pain,
We'd hunt down love together,
Pluck out his flying feather,
And teach his feet a measure,
  And find his mouth a rein;
If you were queen of pleasure,
  And I were king of pain.

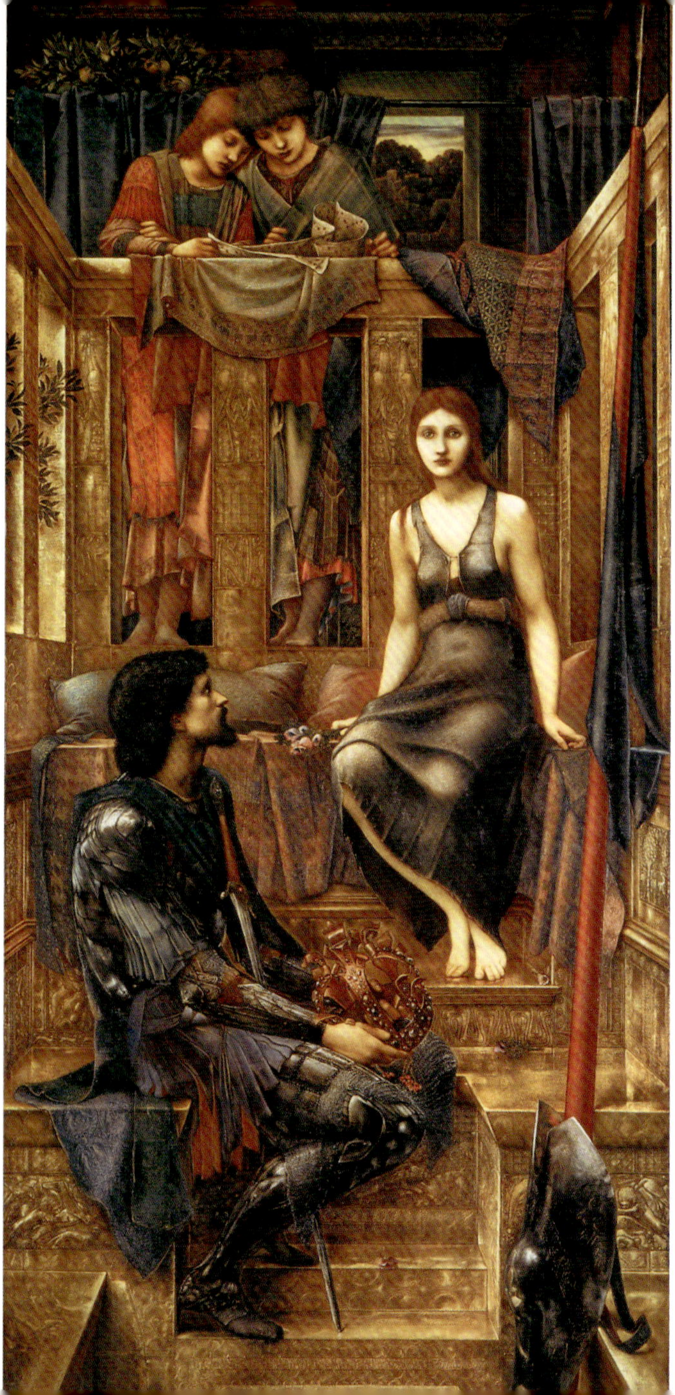

The Beggar Maid

Alfred Tennyson

Her arms across her breast she laid;
   She was more fair than words can say:
Bare-footed came the beggar maid
   Before the king Cophetua.
In robe and crown the king stept down,
   To meet and greet her on her way;
'It is no wonder,' said the lords,
   'She is more beautiful than day.'

As shines the moon in clouded skies,
   She in her poor attire was seen:
One praised her ankles, one her eyes,
   One her dark hair and lovesome mien.
So sweet a face, such angel grace,
   In all that land had never been:
Cophetua swore a royal oath:
   'This beggar maid shall be my queen!'

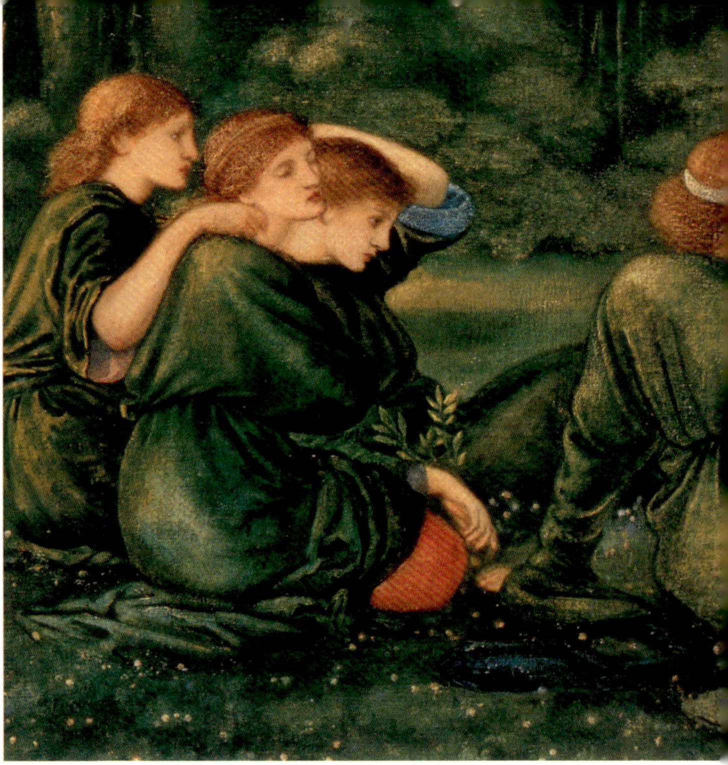

~ Evening ~

John Clare

'Tis evening, the black snail has got on his track,
And gone to its nest is the wren;—
And the packman snail too, with his home on his back;
Clings on the bowed bents like a wen.

The shepherd has made a rude mark with his foot,
Where his shadow reached when he first came;
And it just touched the tree where his secret love cut,
Two letters that stand for love's name.

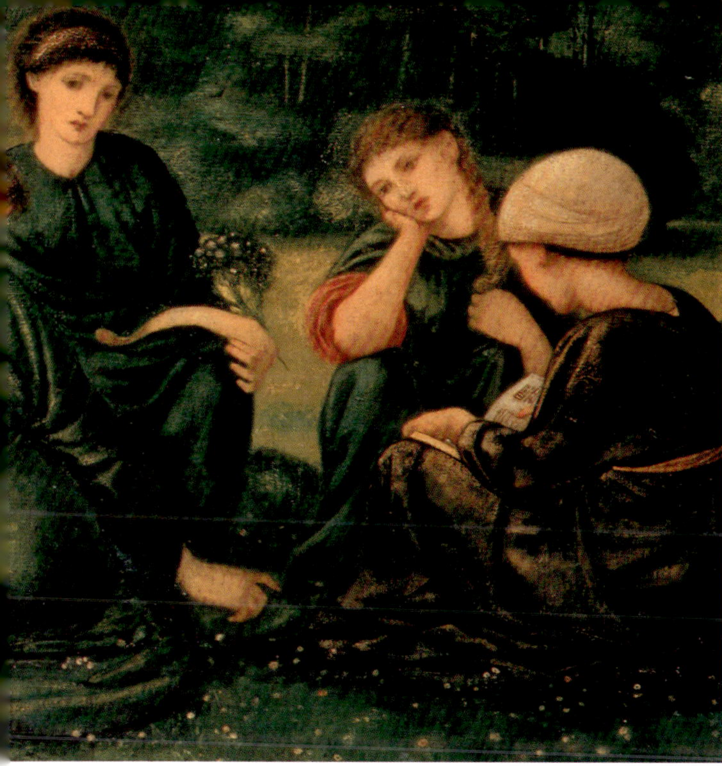

The evening comes in with the wishes of love;—
And the shepherd he looks on the flowers;—
And thinks who would praise the soft song of the dove,
And meet joy in these dewfalling hours.

For nature is love, and the wishers of love;
When nothing can hear or intrude;
It hides from the eagle, and joins with the dove:
In beautiful green solitude.

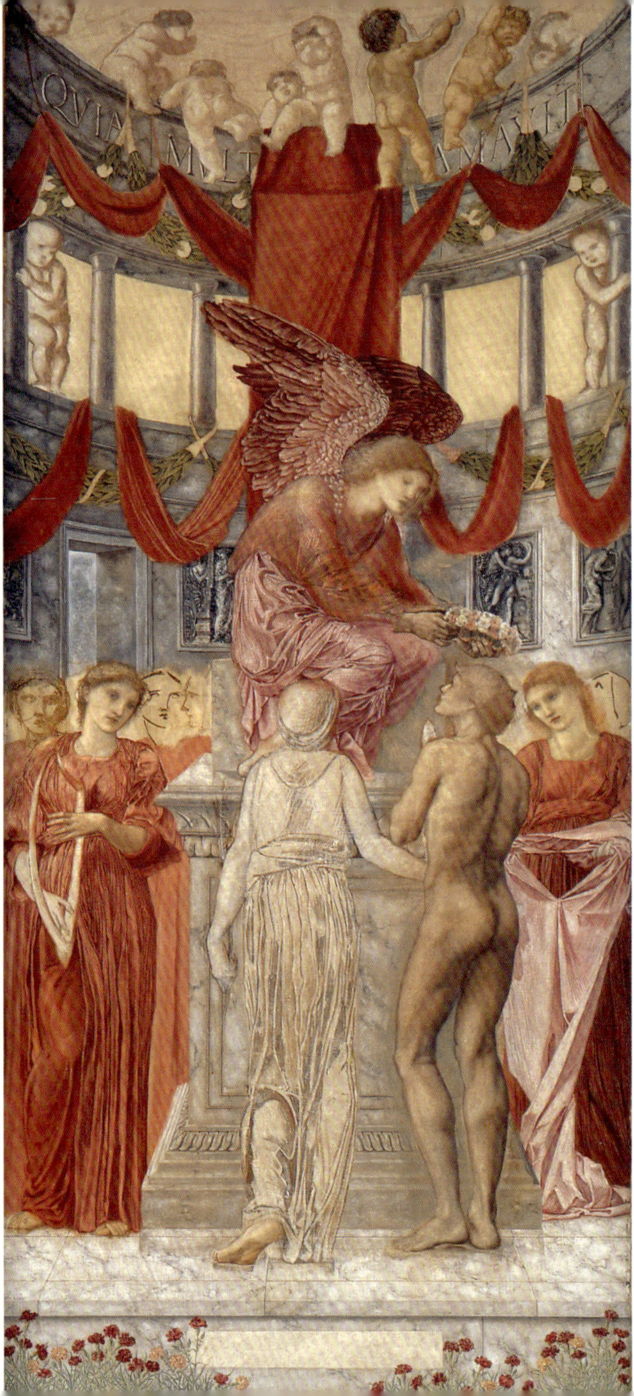
QVIA MVLT AMAVIT

~ Give All to Love ~

Ralph Waldo Emerson

Give all to love;
Obey thy heart;
Friends, kindred, days,
Estate, good fame,
Plans, credit, and the Muse—
Nothing refuse.

'Tis a brave master;
Let it have scope:
Follow it utterly,
Hope beyond hope:
High and more high
It dives into noon,
With wing unspent,
Untold intent;
But it is a god,
Knows its own path,
And the outlets of the sky.

It was never for the mean;
It requireth courage stout,
Souls above doubt,
Valour unbending:
Such 'twill reward;—
They shall return
More than they were,
And ever ascending.

Leave all for love;
Yet, hear me, yet,
One more word thy heart behoved,
One pulse more of firm endeavour—
Keep thee today,
Tomorrow, for ever,
Free as an Arab
Of thy beloved.

Cling with life to the maid;
But when the surprise,
First vague shadow of surmise,
Flits across her bosom young,
Of a joy apart from thee,
Free be she, fancy-free;
Nor thou detain her vesture's hem,
Nor the palest rose she flung
From her summer diadem.

Thou thou loved her as thyself,
As a self of purer clay;
Though her parting dims the day,
Stealing grace from all alive;
Heartily know,
When half-gods go
The gods arrive.

~ Finis ~

Walter Savage Landor

I strove with none, for none was worth my strife:
  Nature I loved, and, next to Nature, Art:
I warmed both hands before the fire of Life;
  It sinks; and I am ready to depart.

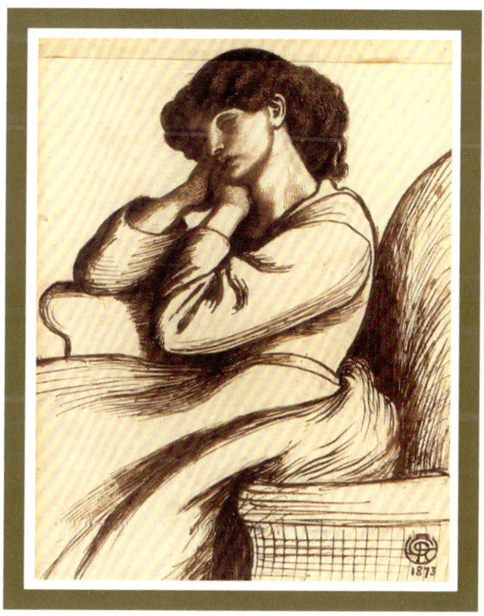

~ Index of Artists and Paintings ~

(The dates of the paintings are given where known)

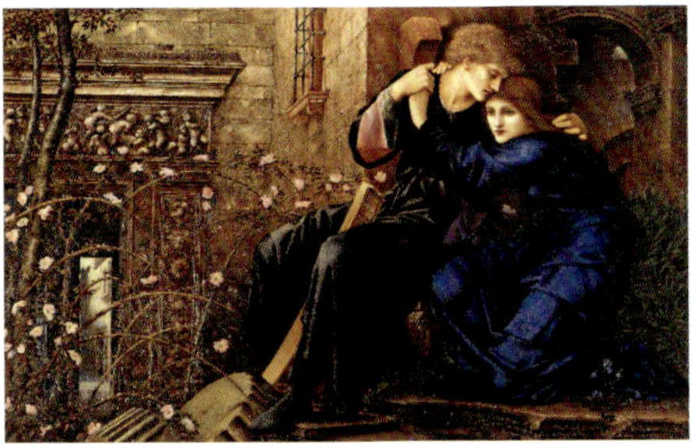

FRONT & BACK COVER AND PAGES 20-21 *above*
Love among the Ruins (1894) *detail*
Sir Edward Burne-Jones (1833-1898)
The National Trust, Wightwick Manor

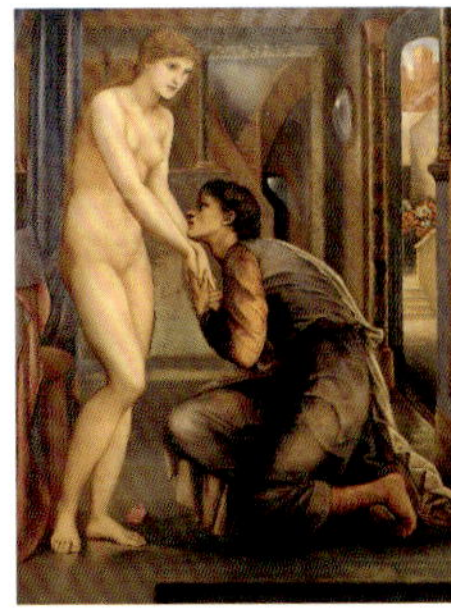

PAGE 5 *above*
Pygmalion and the Image IV:
The Soul Attains (1868-78)
Sir Edward Burne-Jones
Birmingham Museums & Art Gallery

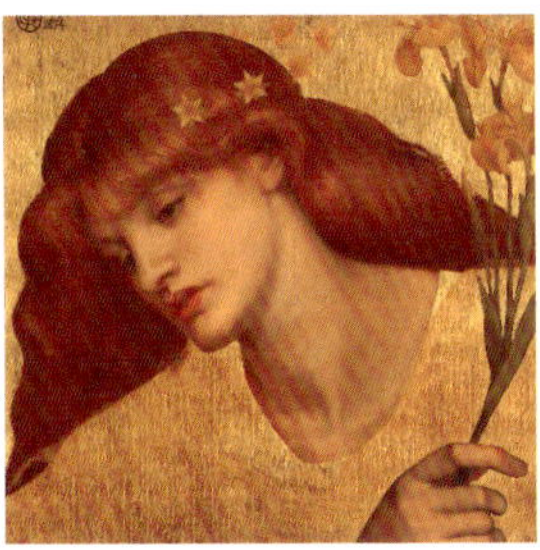

PAGE 9 *left*
Sancta Lilas (1874) *detail*
Dante Gabriel Rossetti
(1828-1882)
Tate Gallery, London

PAGE 10 *right*
The March Marigold
(c.1870) *detail*
Sir Edward Burne-Jones
Piccadilly Gallery, London

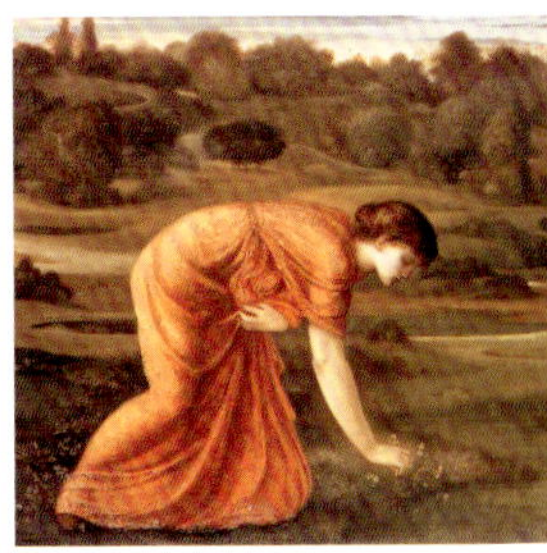

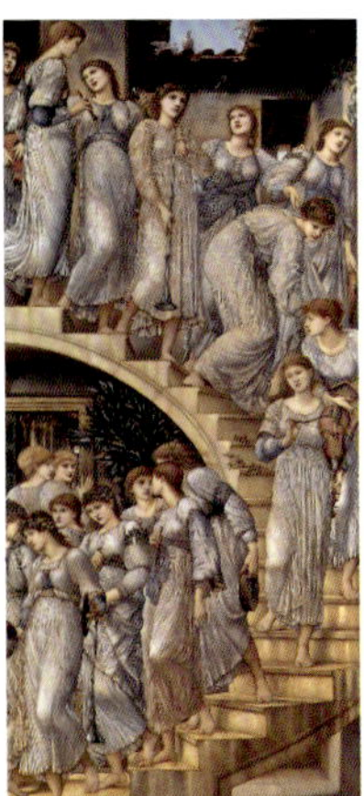

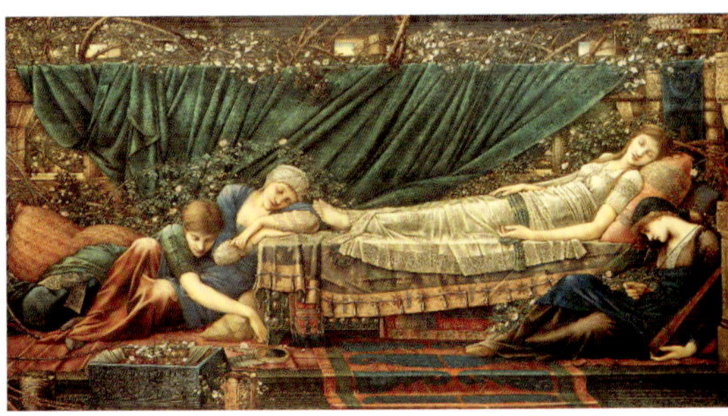

PAGE 13 *left*
The Golden Stairs (1880) *detail*
Sir Edward Burne-Jones
Tate Gallery, London

PAGES 14-15 *above*
The Rose Bower from the Briar Rose
series (1870-90) *detail*
Sir Edward Burne-Jones
Faringdon Collection Trust, Buscot Park

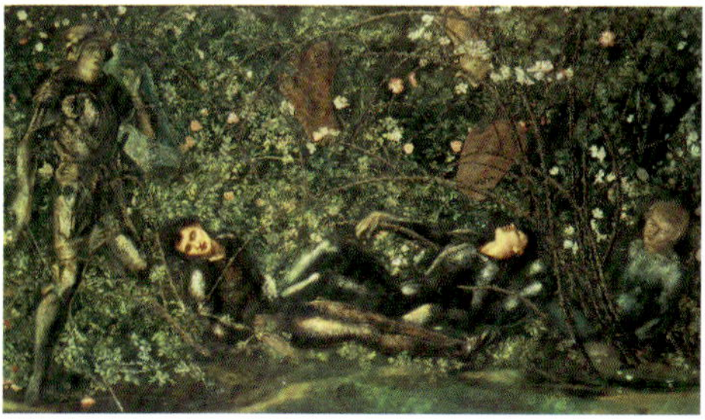

PAGE 16 *above*
The Briar Wood (1869)
detail
Sir Edward Burne-Jones
The Maas Gallery, London

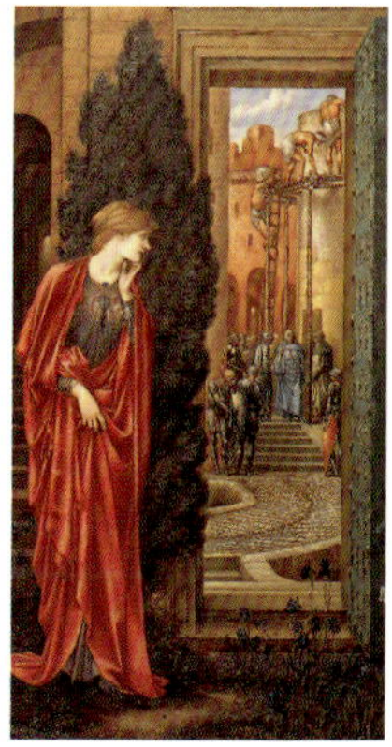

PAGE 19 *right*
Danaë or The Tower of Brass (1887-88)
Sir Edward Burne-Jones
Glasgow Museums: Art Gallery and Museum, Kelvingrove

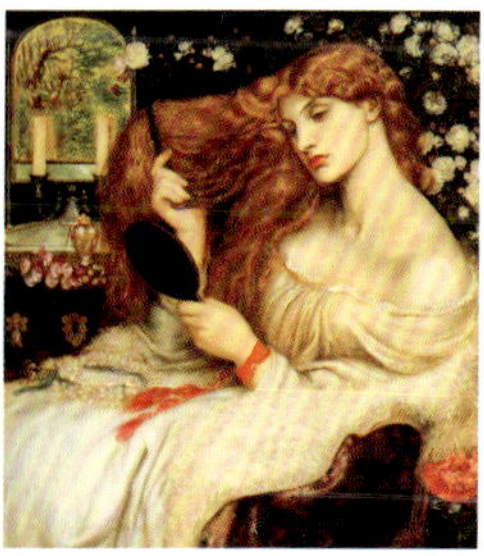

PAGE 23 *left*
Lady Lilith (1864-68)
Dante Gabriel Rossetti
Delaware Art Museum (Samuel and Mary R. Bancroft Memorial, 1935)

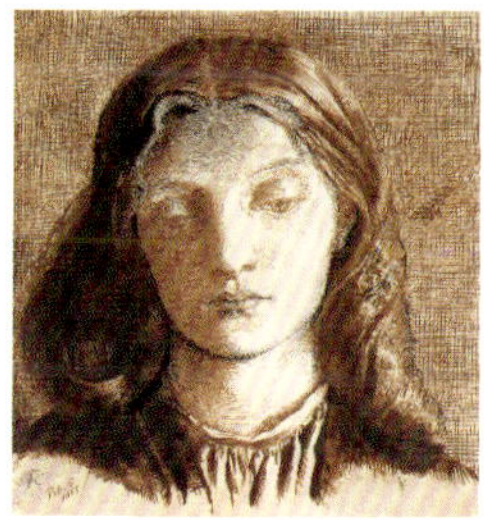

PAGE 24 *right*
Elizabeth Siddal (1855)
Dante Gabriel Rossetti
Ashmolean Museum, Oxford

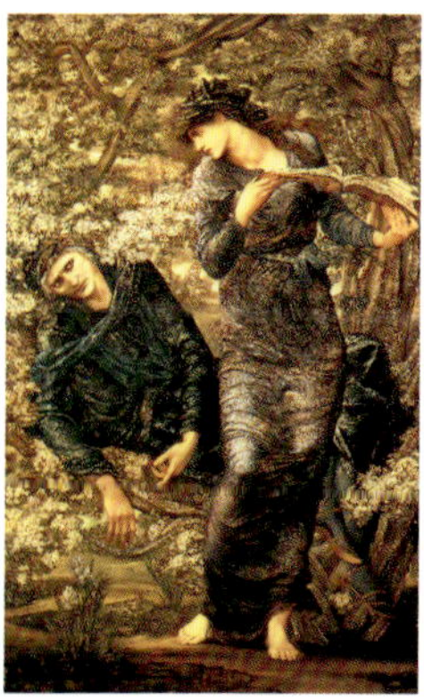

PAGE 27 *above*
The Beguiling of Merlin (1870-74)
detail
Sir Edward Burne-Jones
Lady Lever Art Gallery, Port Sunlight Board of Trustees: National Museums & Galleries on Merseyside

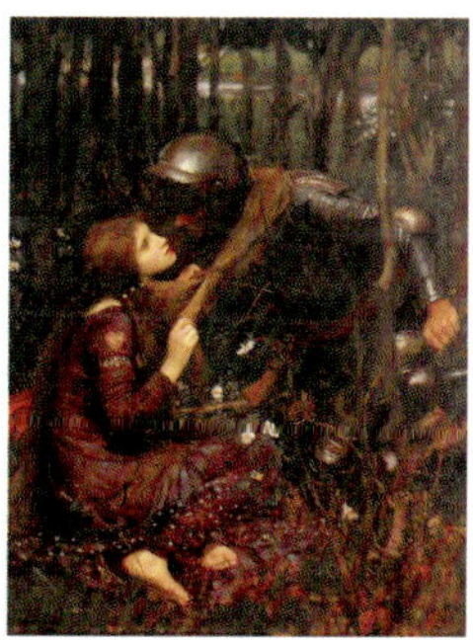

PAGE 28 *above*
La Belle Dame sans Merci (1893) *detail*
John William Waterhouse
(1849-1917)
Hessisches Landesmuseum, Darmstadt

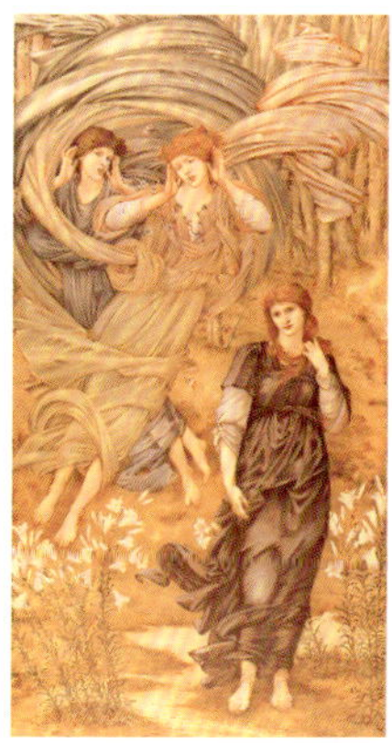

PAGE 33 *above*
Sponsa de Libano (1891)
Sir Edward Burne-Jones
Walker Art Gallery, Liverpool Board of Trustees: National Museums & Galleries on Merseyside

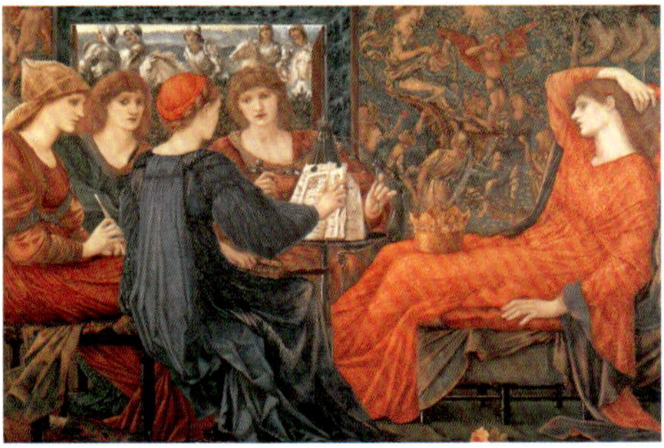

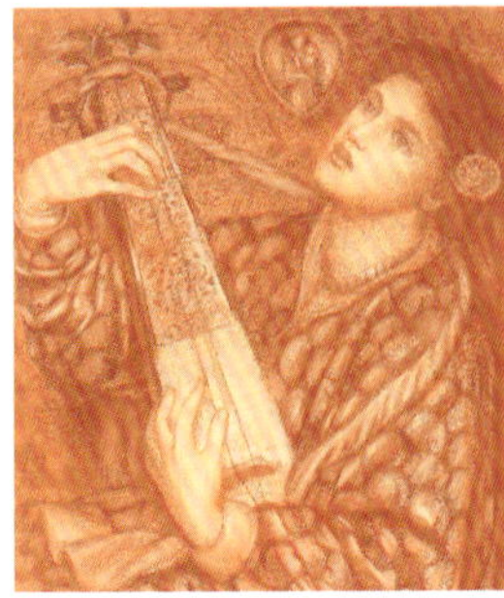

PAGES 34-35 and endpapers *above*
Laus Veneris (1873-75) *detail*
Sir Edward Burne-Jones
Laing Art Gallery, Newcastle-upon-Tyne

PAGE 37 *above*
A Christmas Carol (1867)
Dante Gabriel Rossetti
Private Collection

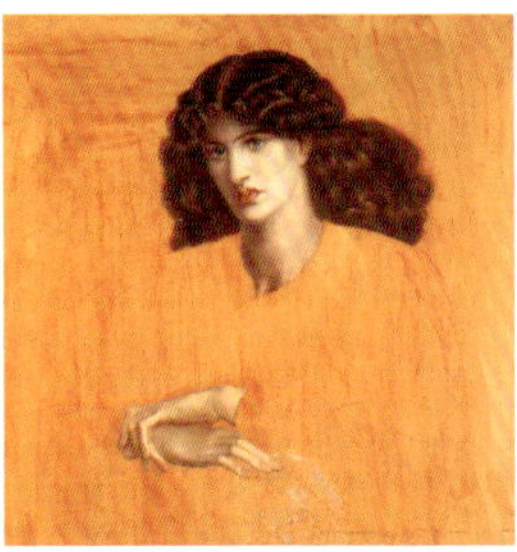

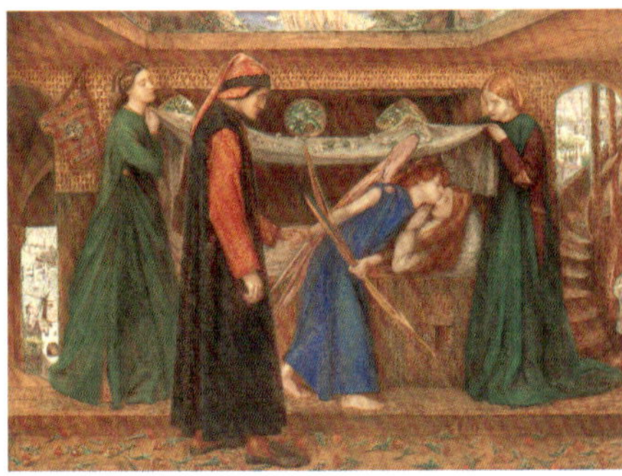

PAGE 39 *above*
Donna della Finestra *detail*
Dante Gabriel Rossetti
Birmingham Museums & Art Gallery

PAGE 40 *above*
Dante's Dream (1856) *detail*
Dante Gabriel Rossetti
Tate Gallery, London

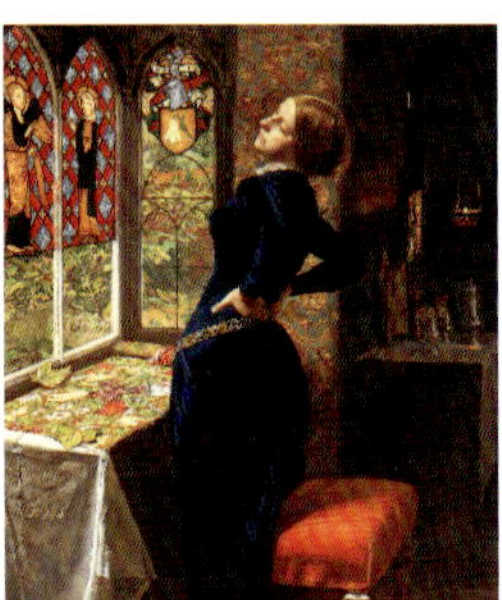

PAGE 43 *left*
Mariana in the Moated Grange (1851) *detail*
Sir John Everett Millais (1829-1896)
The Makins Collection

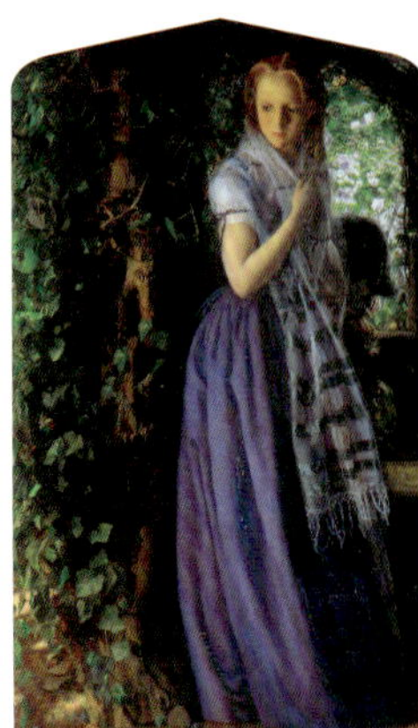

PAGE 44 *right*
April Love (1855-56)
Arthur Hughes (1832-1915)
Tate Gallery, London

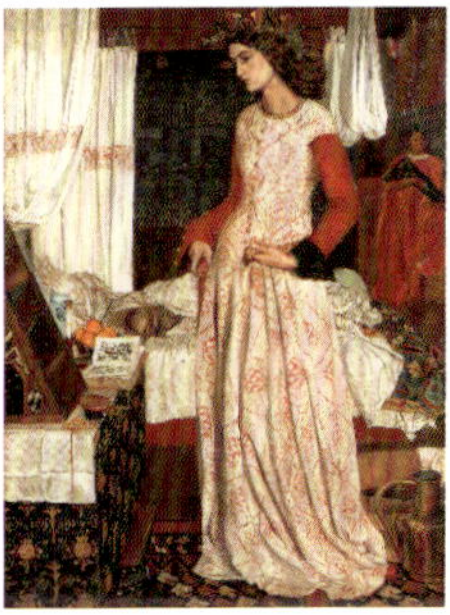

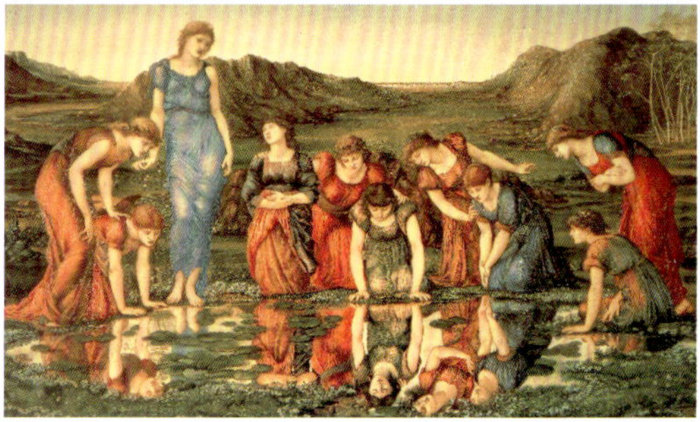

PAGE 47 *above*
La Belle Iseult
William Morris (1834-1896)
Tate Gallery, London

PAGE 49 *above*
The Mirror of Venus (1898)
detail
Sir Edward Burne-Jones
Museu Calouste Gulbenkian, Lisbon

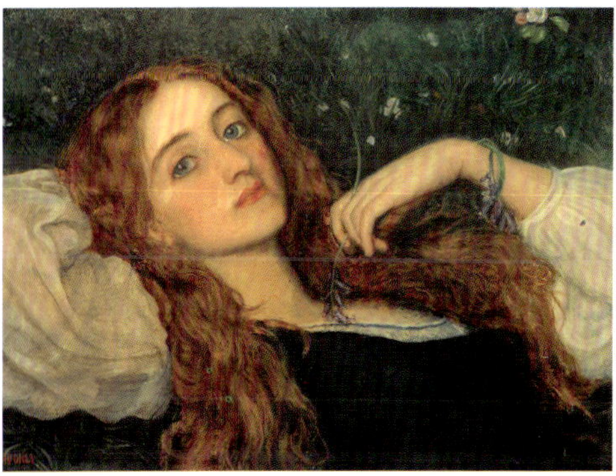

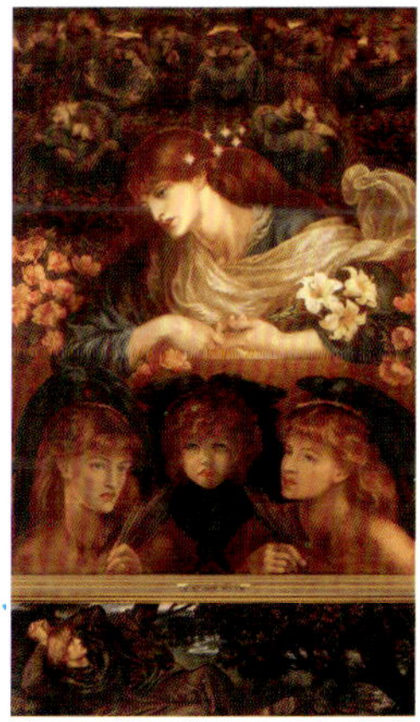

PAGES 53 and 59 (*detail*) *above*
The Blessèd Damozel (1875-78)
Dante Gabriel Rossetti
Fogg Art Museum,
Harvard University Art Museums,
Bequest of Grenville L. Winthrop

PAGE 50 *above*
In the Grass
Arthur Hughes
Sheffield City Art Galleries

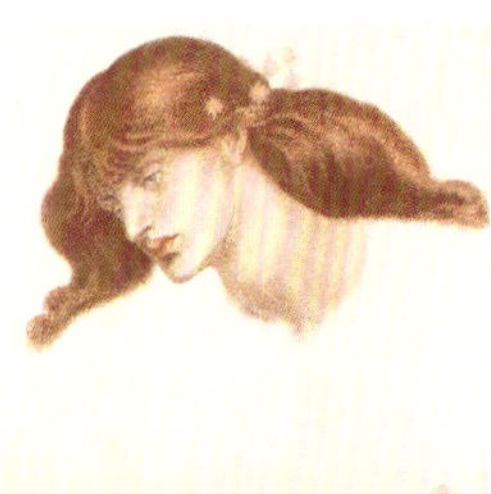

PAGE 57 *left*
Study for the Blessèd Damozel (1876)
Dante Gabriel Rossetti
Manchester City Art Galleries

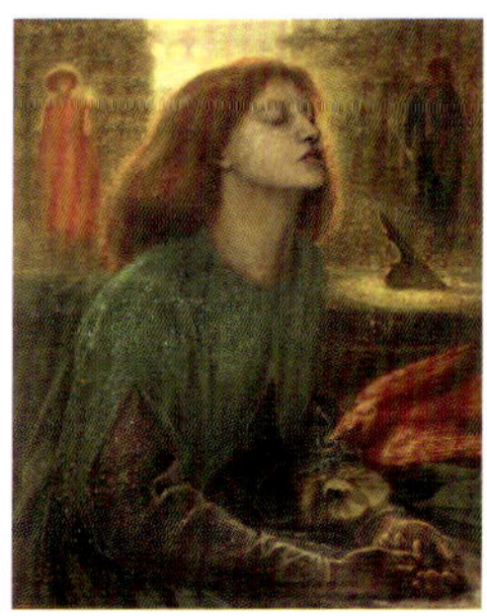

PAGE 60 *right*
Beata Beatrix (1864-70) *detail*
Dante Gabriel Rossetti
Tate Gallery, London

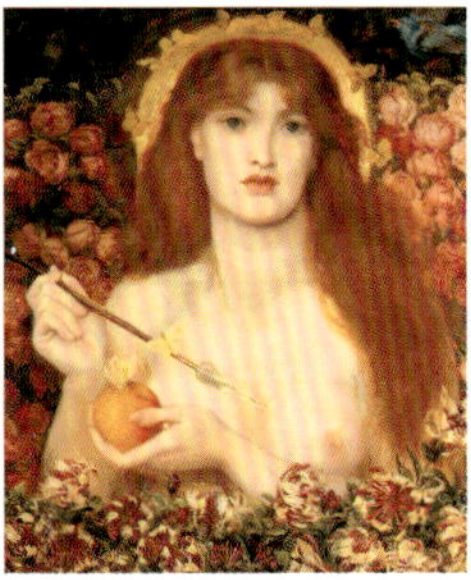

PAGE 63 *left*
Venus Verticordia (1864-68)
Dante Gabriel Rossetti
Russell-Cotes Art Gallery and Museum, Bournemouth

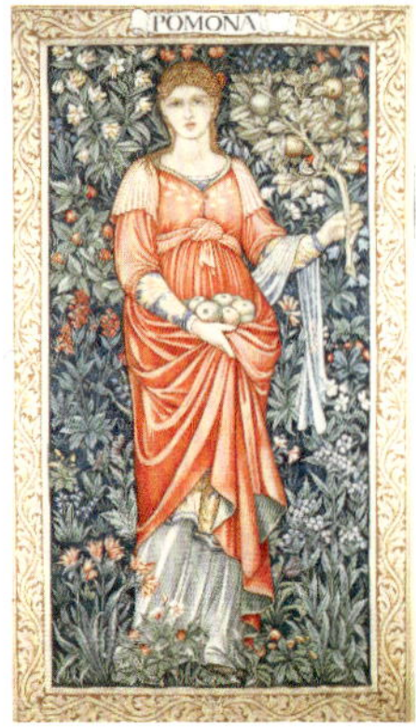

PAGE 64 *above*
Pomona
Sir Edward Burne-Jones,
(tapestry made by Morris & Co. c.1885)
Harris Museum and Art Gallery, Preston, Lancashire

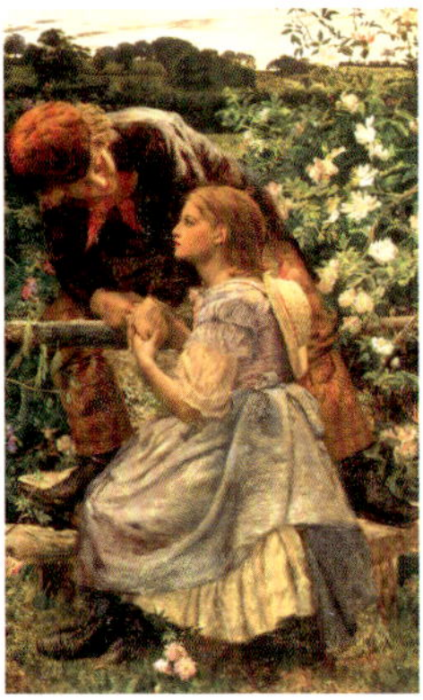

PAGE 67 *above*
Early Lovers (1858)
Frederick Smallfield (1829-1915)
Manchester City Art Galleries

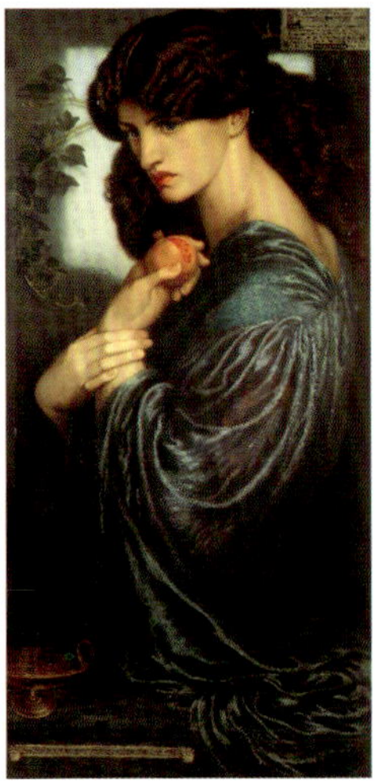

PAGE 69 *left*
Proserpine (1874)
Dante Gabriel Rossetti
Tate Gallery, London

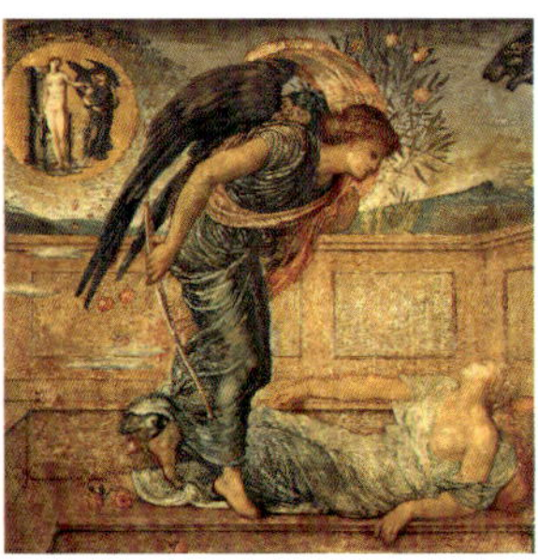

PAGE 70 *above*
Cupid Finding Psyche Asleep by a Fountain *detail*
Sir Edward Burne-Jones
Birmingham Museums & Art Gallery

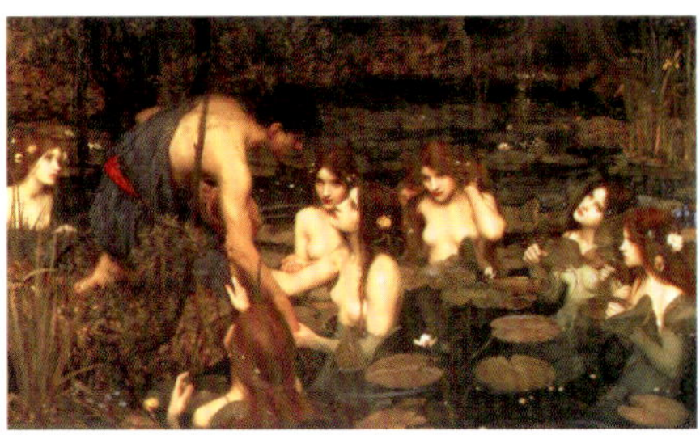

PAGE 72 *above*
Hylas and the Nymphs (1896) *detail*
John William Waterhouse
Manchester City Art Galleries

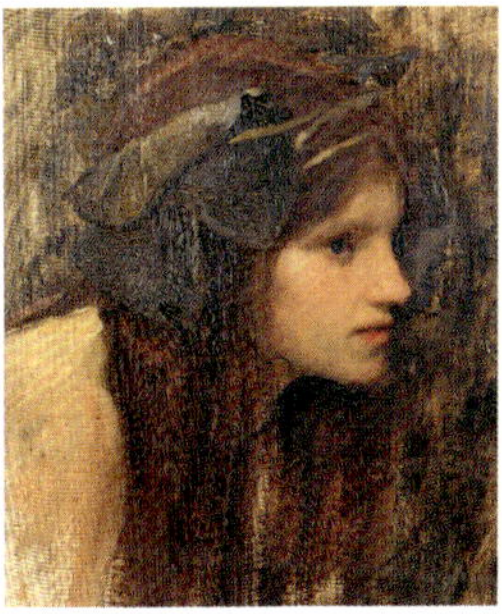

PAGE 74 *above*
A Study for a Naiad
John William Waterhouse
Bonhams, London

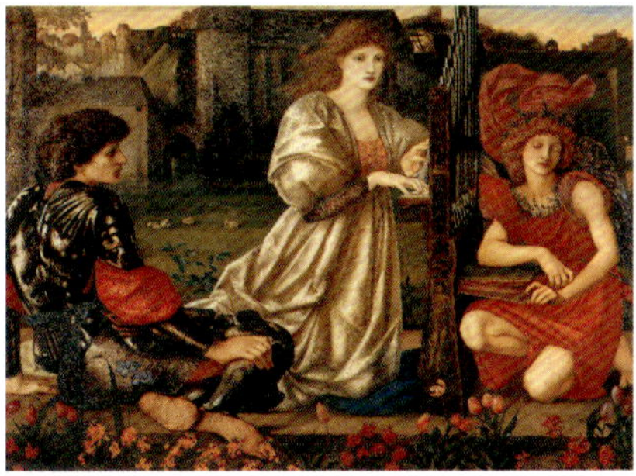

PAGES 76-77 *above*
The Love Song
Sir Edward Burne-Jones
The Metropolitan Museum of Art, New York
The Alfred N. Punnett Endowment Fund, 1947 (47.26)

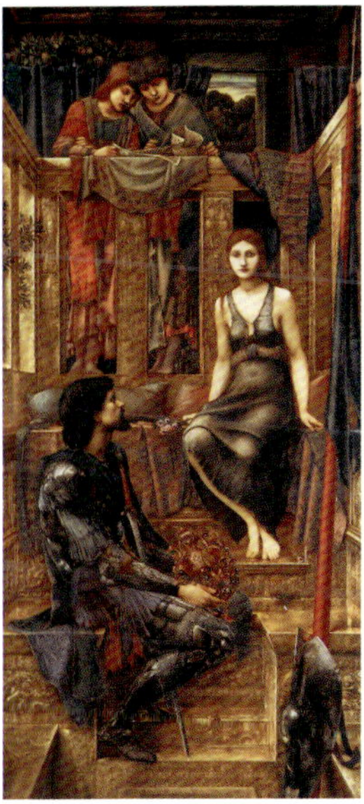

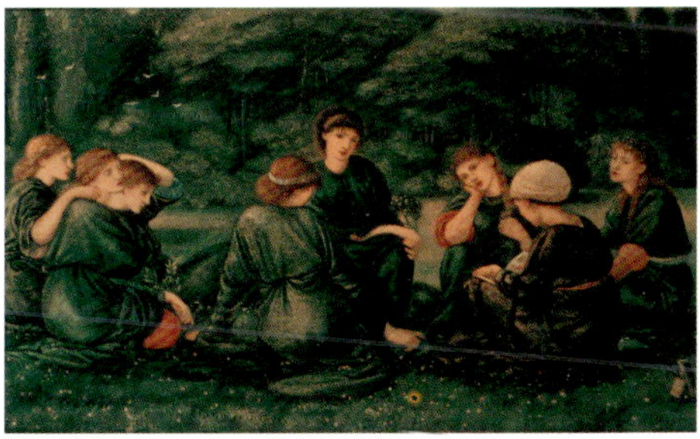

PAGES 80-81 *above*
Green Summer (1868) *detail*
Sir Edward Burne-Jones
Christie's Images

PAGE 85 *below*
Mrs William Morris (1873)
Dante Gabriel Rossetti
Private Collection

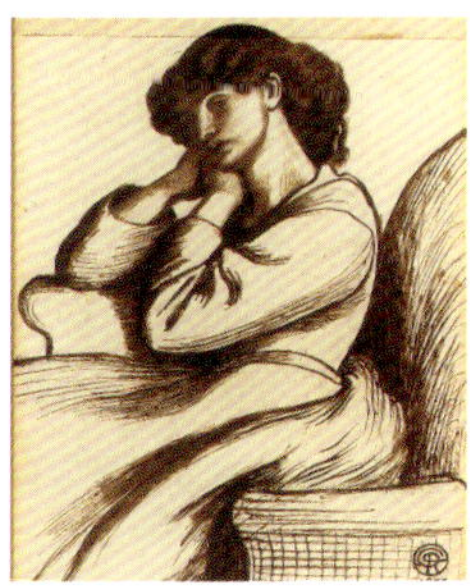

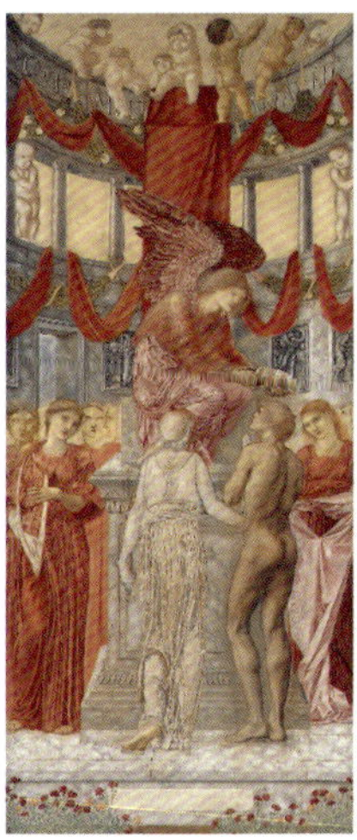

PAGE 78 *above*
King Cophetua and the Beggar Maid (1884)
Sir Edward Burne-Jones
Tate Gallery, London

PAGE 82 *right*
The Temple of Love
Sir Edward Burne-Jones
Tate Gallery, London

Index of Poetry

PHOTOGRAPHIC ACKNOWLEDGEMENTS

For permission to reproduce the paintings on the following pages and for supplying photographs, the Publishers would like to thank:

Birmingham Museums & Art Gallery: 5, 39, 70
Bridgeman Art Library: 10, 16, 24, 27, 28, 33, 34-35, 43, 49, 50, 63, 64, 67, 72, 74, 80-81, endpapers
Delaware Art Museum: 23
Faringdon Collection Trust: 14-15
Courtesy of the Fogg Art Museum, Harvard University Art Museums: 53, 59
Glasgow Museums: Art Gallery and Museum, Kelvingrove: 19
© Manchester City Art Galleries: 57
The Metropolitan Museum of Art: 76-77
National Trust Photographic Library/Derrick E. Witty: front & back cover, 20-21
Sotheby's Picture Library: 37, 85
© Tate Gallery, London: 9, 13, 40, 44, 47, 60, 69, 78, 82

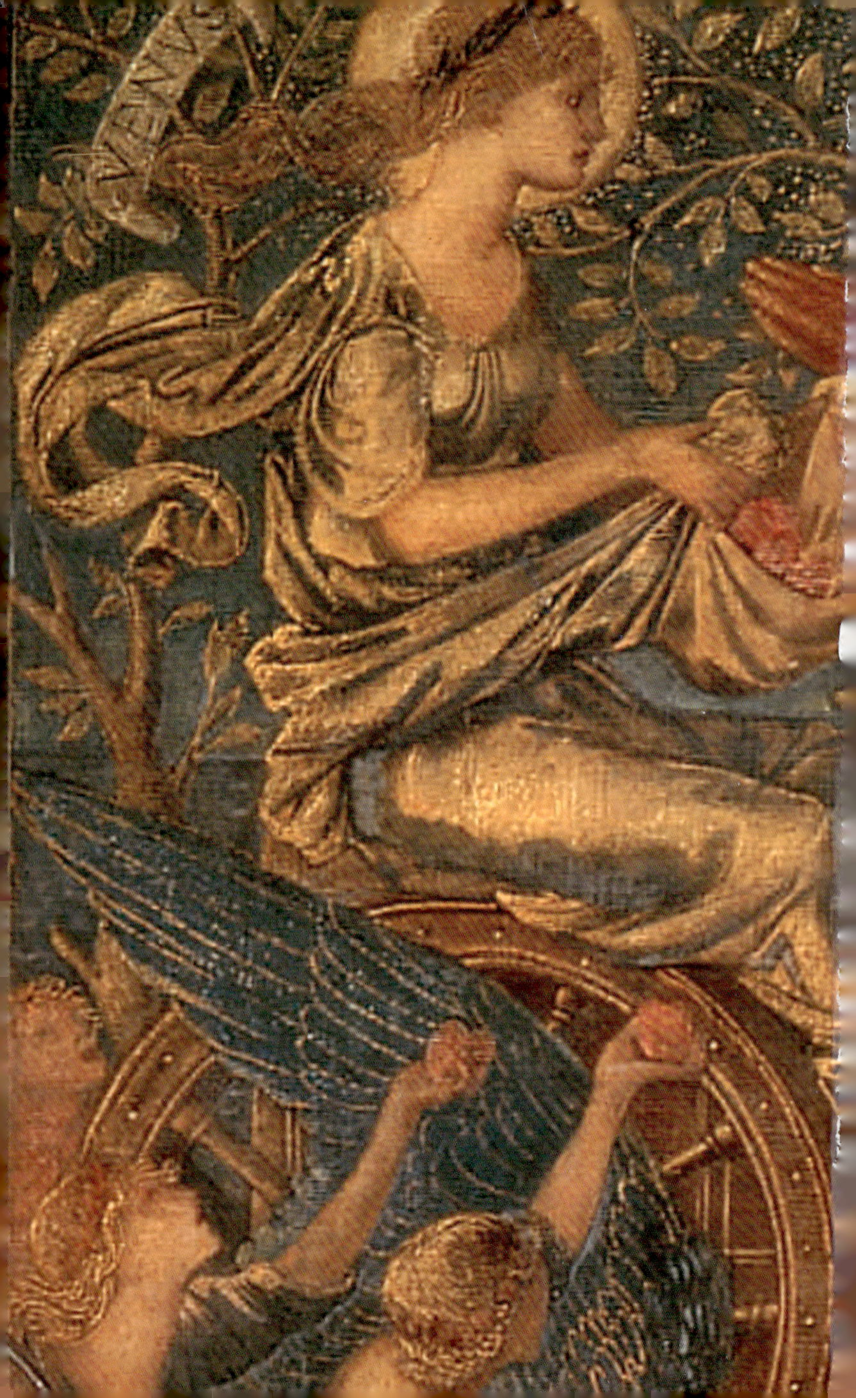